D1468503

CANDYLAND

For the Progression of Human Evolution

Kyle D. Jones

Candyland

© 2015 Kyle D. Jones

Editing by © Kristen Corrects, Inc.

Manufactured in the United States of America

First Printing, 2015

On-Demand Publishing LLC, part of the Amazon group of companies.

100 Enterprise Way, Scotts Valley, CA 95066

ISBN-13: 978-1514372760
ISBN-10: 1514372762

"When you grow up you tend to get told the world is the way it is and to live your life inside the world. Try not to bash into the walls too much. Try to have a nice family, have fun, save a little money. That's a very limited life. Life can be much broader once you discover one simple fact:

Everything around you that you call life was made up by people that were no smarter than you and you can change it, you can influence it, you can build your own things that other people can use. Once you learn that, you'll never be the same again."

— Steve Jobs (1955-2011)

I dedicate this book to all of the human species with joy, appreciation, and love.

Acknowledgements

My Loving Family

Erin Guiney

Vivien Makhoul

Brenna Flatley

Tyler Davis

Keenan Doricent

Franki Deckert

The Chapman Family

Gillian Childers

Austin Collins

Andrew Crumley

Devon Mayfield

Abigail Bennett

Chris Johnson

Emily Rooks

Morgan Elliott

Thank you for accepting me through such a difficult phase in my life and accepting me for who I have become. I could never fully express how much it means to me.

Peace. Love. Blessings.

Contents

Introduction to Candyland

Since scientists have developed the ability to decipher the genome and compare the genetic composition of various species, they have learned that nearly 98.5% of the genes in humans and chimpanzees are impossible to tell apart. It does not mean that human beings have directly evolved from chimpanzees, but it does mean that we have descended from the same ancestor. The molding of our body, shape of our hands, structuring of our brain, and way of locomotion can all be traced back to primates that existed millions of years ago in forest of present day Africa and Europe. According to evolutionary biologist, Neil Shubin, our coccyx—tailbone—represents the tails we used to have millions of years ago.

Scientific research estimates that Earth itself is approximately 4.55 billion years old, and the human species has only existed for a tiny portion of its existence. Paleontologists believe that the earliest hominid species—members of the primate family

b

that can move about on two legs—diverged from the ape lineage between 5 and 8 million years ago. Years later, the oldest humanlike fossil was discovered in Ethiopia, dated at 4.4 million years old. However, according to Max Planck Institute for Evolutionary Anthropology, our species of **homo sapiens sapiens**—the modern day human—is only about 40,000 years old.

Despite our short time on Earth we have evolved far beyond any other living entity. Over time, we have developed color vision, a voice box, ability to store memories, an individual consciousness, strength to stand upright on two feet, and an increase in brain size. Each of our evolutionary developments has occurred due to changes in the environment, allowing us to survive and reproduce.

Our most important evolutionary development is our increased brain size because it has allowed us to develop an imagination. Though it is a beautiful thing to have an imagination, we have used it in many destructive ways. We have used our imagination as a means of dehumanizing each individual soul. Instead of coming into the physical world and being told that society is already involved in an illusionary game that has derived from the human imagination, we treat it as if life is supposed to be this way. Individuals are led to journey through the human experience mindless to their purpose of coming into the physical world to further the evolutionary process.

Calendars, clocks, clothes, names, money, jobs, school, politics, marriage, advanced technology, houses, cars, and societal expectations are all illusions that have derived from the human imagination, dehumanizing the individual soul from fully experiencing the beauty of the human form. The more we detach ourselves from these beautiful, but destructive ideologies, the more we can free ourselves from the various detriments of ignorance and cherish the bliss of the physical world. Detaching ourselves from these ideologies does not mean completely removing these subjects from our lives, but it is a better method to not letting them distract us from our higher self and ability to see equality in each living entity. We can no longer look at each other for our material possessions and physical differences, but instead as equal, individual souls that have

d

manifested into an outer shell for a temporary existence.

The creation of organized religion has also derived from the human imagination, giving individuals a sense of spirituality. As we are naturally spiritual beings, we can only evolve by having our own spiritual experience rather than completely dedicating our lives to studying those of individuals that have existed before us. We do not consciously realize that Jesus, Buddha, and Muhammad were not religious individuals, but spiritual philosophers that taught the love of self and love of humanity. Generation after generation has passed down the beautiful stories of these ancient spiritual philosophers as a source of inspiration, however, over time, a few money hungry individuals have used them as a means of corruption and destruction. These stories have been molded into religious doctrines, used as a means of blinding the individual soul from its purpose of coming into the physical world, mentally enslaving the human mind to the biases of society.

By taking control of our own individual spiritual journey, we can transition back to a stream of higher consciousness, which is the state of being we are in at birth, before we encounter the illusions of the physical world. This state of being has been diminished through the labeling of external subjects and collective beliefs. It is in this state of being that we understand everything is a vibration and that our purpose of coming to the physical environment is to further the evolutionary process. However, the diminishing of our stream of higher consciousness has led us to believe that we are five-sensory beings rather than multi-sensory beings, causing us to think that the purpose of the human experience is to acquire material possessions—money, cars, clothes, and other superficial human creations—rather than furthering the evolutionary process.

According to Edward H. Hagen, an American anthropologist that contributes to the field of evolutionary psychology, the human species has not evolved for more than 10,000 years. A natural resource stock check made by the British Broadcasting Corporation in June 2012 shows that the Earth has at most 80 years of non-renewable natural resources remaining. The stock check also predicts that the coral reefs will be diminished by

f

INTRODUCTION

2100, and the Amazon Rain Forest will be completely deforested by the year of 2208. With this being the case, our species must become enlightened to access the next realm of consciousness necessary for the furthering of our evolutionary process, allowing us to survive and prosper without the subjects we rely on in the present moment.

Due to each individual soul having an individual consciousness, we can only further evolve our species through a collective consciousness. We have to collectively ascend from the low vibrational frequency of fear to the high vibrational frequency of enlightenment. This will make all technological progress and economic systems completely dismissed. Humanity will cross over from an egocentric, material life to an egoless, loving, spiritual life. British journalist, Graham Hancock, believes that this is the Heaven that the Bible refers to, accessing the next realm of consciousness through the furthering of the evolutionary process, allowing us to live in a permanent state of peace, bliss, and love.

In this book, I list principles of individuality that I believe are most important to the individual soul in the conditioned higher civilization. Modern day higher civilizations have become too attached to the illusions of the physical world to completely remove them from their way of thinking. However, through individualism—the belief that the needs of each individual are more important than the needs of the society—and each individual cherishing their individuality, we can still reach a level of enlightenment. Individuality allows us to be our true self—the individual we were manifested to be in the physical world—and journey through the human experience from within. Despite our physical differences and societal labels, we will be able to appreciate and cherish each other as One. It is the realization of Oneness—all living entities, including each human being, and God are interconnected beyond the outer shell—that will allow us to ascend to a higher realm of consciousness, furthering our evolutionary process.

A brief description to how the Universe works can also be found in this book, allowing us to see how powerful we are as beings in the human form despite society's dehumanization. Too many individuals are lost in the world and blind to the

h

INTRODUCTION

powerful Universe that allows the world to exist. By awakening to these Universal principles, our life will be transformed, positively changing the way we journey through the human experience.

PART I.

FOR THE SOCIETY: INDIVIDUALITY: SELF-LOVE, SELF-PERCEPTION, SELF- DOUBT, SELF-RESPECT, SELF-PROGRESSION

Individuality

"The greatest fear people have is that of being themselves. They want to be 50 Cent or someone else. They do what everyone else does even if it doesn't fit where and who they are But you get nowhere that way; your energy is weak and no one pays attention to you." — *50 Cent*

NEARLY TWO THOUSANDS YEARS AGO, human beings created the compass, lever, and mirror. One thousand years ago, human beings created toothpaste, parachutes, and mechanical clocks. During the 1800s, human creations such as the automobile, light bulb, and telephone blessed the world. Why is this important? Because year after year, decade after decade, century after century there has been individuals that followed their heart and paved their own path, impacting the world in many powerful ways.

These individuals were creative thinkers, inventors, artists, and philosophers that had to endure various forms of hatred, discouragement, and deep scrutiny. Despite what these individuals endured on their journey through the human experience, they continued following the path that their heart led them on to achieve success. Each of these individuals realized that we come into and leave this beautiful world alone. They realized that the legacy each of us leaves behind is all that matters in the end—when our job, our bank account, our level of education, and our material possessions no longer exist. Steve Jobs, Tupac Shakur, Martin Luther King, Isaac Newton, and Albert Einstein are textbook examples of individuals that have died but left their legacies behind on Earth. Their names, inventions, and unique thought processes will never die because they followed their heart without conforming to popular opinion and the negative energy of their peers.

Presently, in the 15th year of the 21st century, the majority of us have strayed away from following our heart. We have started to neglect our individual pursuits of happiness and settle for lives society perceives as normal. We slave in jobs we do not enjoy and work long hours only for the want of money and material things. Most individuals in the society hate Mondays because they hate what they do on Mondays and love the weekends because they get to live life, the "perfect getaway."

It is time that we awaken to the truth of our existence and cherish our individuality. We were not born into the physical world to follow a system other human beings created, enslaved by clocks and calendars. Each of us has distinct thoughts, talents, ideas, and gifts to share with the world. Too many of us neglect our individuality and let the fear of being shunned by society lead us into settling for a life opposite of the life we desire deep in our heart.

As a society, we have become bombarded by the subconscious illusion of perceiving being shunned and alone as a bad thing. We spend most of our life resisting loneliness and become miserable fitting into an image that does not represent who we are as an individual soul. Deep in our heart, beyond the illusions we are blinded by, we are aware of the bigness of our being and its inability to fit into any societal label or box. However, instead of following our intuition, we find it easier to conform to the man-made society, falling victim to our fear of being alone and neglecting to follow the path of the Universe within to fulfill our life purpose.

Once we learn to cherish our individuality and find comfort in our inner being, we will see the beauty of being alone. Loneliness is an illusion that exists due to the way our minds have been conditioned to think by societal biases. Truthfully, we are never lonely because we walk with the Universe that lives within each of us on our journey from birth to death. Most individuals feel lonely because they go their whole life without going within, attempting to control external situations. By neglecting to go within, we will never have the confidence to embrace our individuality and be ourself in a world that glorifies fitting in.

Our mind, heart, and soul are all qualities of our individuality; the Creator of the Universe did not create us with these qualities as a collective. When we cherish our individuality, we think and act from our individual judgment rather than thinking and acting for the approval of others. We live for internal achievements rather than societal achievements. We require independence from others rather than wasting energy depending on others. Without cherishing our individuality in a world that forces conformity, we will never reach our full potential or further evolve our being.

Many great accomplishments in all the years of human existence have derived from the independent, individual mind. On the contrary, many forms of destruction have derived from attempts of forcing humanity into an assembly of programmed individuals that lack belief in individual rights and individual thought processes. Minor happenings in history such as the enslavement of foreign beings, mass genocide of natives, and murderous hatred of the "Other" are all instances of the individual being neglected. To promote the power of the individual mind, we must neglect these destructive practices and examine ways to nourish the beliefs of individual rights and individual thought processes.

Our home, the United States of America, was originally fashioned around principles of individualism and the alienable rights of the individual. Once a nation where the individual was free to seek bliss; to create, not to give up, to thrive, not to starve, to accomplish, and not settle. We have slowly become a country suffering from self-sacrifice and fabricated happiness.

Things such as truth, freedom, and unity have become unimportant to the leaders of the world; greed, power, and control have become the primary. The world has become a place where the majority supports conformity, the minority—individuals that faithfully cherish their individuality—are abandoned, and human beings are systematized around the institutional imperative of collecting capital to survive. Along with conformity came sickening habits of nationalism, racism, monitoring of populations, and the development of popular opinion.

The general public has become so consumed by popular opinion that these popular opinions are mistaken as truth, corrupting the mind of both future and current generations. The majority of us have been led to think that there is a right or wrong way to journey through the human experience, but this way of thinking is distorted. The idea of there being a right and wrong has become established through the falsified conditioning and brainwashing of the human mind. By transitioning back to individualism and a world that strongly cherishes their individuality, the illusion of right and wrong will cease to exist.

Individualism brings acceptance, love, and respect for all individuals regardless the color of their skin, quality of their clothes, and size of their home. With individualism, the fear of being judged, fear of appearing awkward, and fear of sounding crazy would not exist. These ways of being only exist due to the stream of lower consciousness most individuals in the society have. We are no longer conscious to the truth of our being, understanding that we are all individuals born to be unique and bring our individual gifts into the world.

The objective of this section in my work of art, Candyland, is to encourage change. Not only for the betterment of the world but also for the emotional and mental health of the individual. In the present world, change is perceived as negative; it is perceived as fake or phony. This negative perception of change is the reason most individuals are trapped in a life of self-denial. Truthfully, change is growth and growth is the core of our being.

Mahatma Gandhi once quoted, "You must be the change you want to see in the world." We must take this quote into consideration as we begin to cherish our individuality and neglect following what is viewed as popular and normal. The desire to feel accepted has wrecked the world and robbed billions of individuals from reaching their full potential. As human beings, we are more powerful than our minds have been conditioned to think. Believing that we have no power over what happens in the world and its construction is a horrible way of thinking.

Affirmations are listed at the end of each chapter to assist in changing our thought process into a more prosperous and positive state. When we say these affirmations, we cannot just say them; we have to feel, believe, and embody what we are affirming out to the

Universe. Each affirmation should be spoken out loud while looking in the mirror at least three times a day for thirty seconds each. The more we practice the affirmations listed, the more we manifest the ways of being we are affirming into our life.

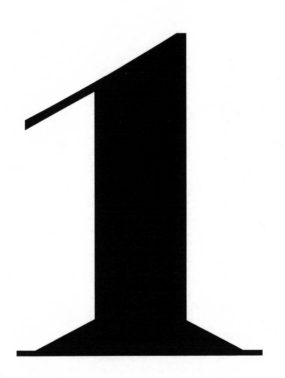

The Open Secret (Self-Love)

"Love is not just a verb, it is you looking in the mirror." — *Kendrick Lamar*

THE FOUNDER OF PSYCHOSYNTHESIS—a concept characterized by our natural tendency to evolve and improve our personal development—Roberto Assagioli, once stated, "Ninety-five percent of our energy is spent protecting, defending, and maintaining our identity." We get so consumed by the external world that we neglect the Universe within. The conditioning of society has diminished our higher consciousness, as we no longer realize we are whole, unique, and created through the process of love.

What is love? This is a question that receives more than seven billion dissimilar answers. The Ancient Greeks believed that there were four various forms of love:

EROS

The representations of love portrayed to the masses through movies, music, and other societal outlets are Eros. Eros is the form of love that is dramatic. It is an obsession rather than actual true, unconditional love. Individuals that love from a state of Eros start off madly in love but eventually become extremely destructive toward each other. Shakespeare's *Romeo and Juliet* is an example of Eros.

PHILIA

Philia means close friendship or brotherly love in Greek. It is the kind of love that we have toward family members, friends, co-workers, and neighbors. The love found in most teenage relationships are also representations of Philia. Ancient philosopher, Aristotle, talks about Philia in his work of art, the Nicomachean Ethics, which expresses how men should live. Like Eros,

Philia is not a representation of true, unconditional love; it is more of a common societal expression.

STORGE

Storge is the kind of love that comes with familiarity. The love family members have for each other is Storge. It has nothing to do with the external or internal characteristics of another individual; it simply exists due to being familiar with someone else. The movie, *Love & Basketball*, is an example of Storge.

AGAPE

Agape refers to a deep, powerful, true, and unconditional love. Possessiveness, jealousy, fear, and need are nonexistent to the individual loving in an Agape way. The spiritual philosopher, Jesus Christ, lived out of Agape by sacrificing himself for the sins of the world. Of the four forms of love the Ancient Greeks believed, Agape is described as the finest and truest of them all.

Despite the four Ancient Greek interpretations of love, which are genius interpretations of love by the means of society, love cannot be defined by words or described as any societal experience. Love is a feeling, a state of being, and the only expression the Creator—God—has manifested into the physical world. There is not one subject in the Universe that is not made of love, including our very being.

We have become so consumed by the idea of getting married and spending our life with another individual that we have developed a distorted perception of love. The ideology of marriage is a man-made creation created for the sole purpose of assisting the individual with an improved chance of physical survival. With marriage, we become more capable of maintaining food, water, shelter, and health in the society. However, the title of husband and wife does not signify love. Love cannot be forced or established as legitimate by government documentation, agreeing to be with another individual until death does part.

It is when we find clarity—discover our purpose of coming into the physical world—and love ourself that we become open to experiencing true, unconditional love. Without loving ourself, we will constantly feel the need to get married and have someone external of our being to make us feel complete. Without loving ourself, we will constantly feel the urge to fit in and follow the crowd due to the overwhelming fear of being judged by others, making it impossible to cherish our individuality. When we are not bringing love to our own being, we look to an external source for reassurance and a sense of love.

The longer we allow our ability to love who we are to be based upon what other individuals think of us, the longer it will take to live a happy, blessed, and prosperous life. Just because someone stops loving us does not mean we should stop loving ourself. Just because someone does not believe in us does not mean we should stop believing in ourself. Just because someone thinks we hold no value in the world does not mean we should believe we hold no value in the world.

Our existence and manifestation into the physical world is enough to show us that we are worthy of love. We should not need other individuals to comment on our social media post to feel deserving and worthy of love. We should not need a girlfriend or boyfriend to tell us that we are beautiful to feel and believe that we are beautiful. We should not need the nicest cars, houses, and clothes to love who we are. Any form of love that is not coming from within our being is a false representation of love that can be taken away from us any second of our life, leading us back to the one thing we have control over, ourself.

When love and fulfillment are not coming from within our own heart and soul, we live life from an unconscious state of self-hatred—lack of self-love. Individuals that have another girlfriend or boyfriend or start partying immediately after they get out of a relationship live life from an unconscious state of self-hatred. Individuals that feel the need to constantly wear makeup and fantasize over material possessions live life from an unconscious state of self-hatred. These individuals live life blind to the Universe that exists within their being.

Self-hatred is the root of all evil and wrongdoing in the world. It is the reason we believe that "it's a dog-eat-dog world," and that it is necessary to take advantage of others. It is the reason millions of individuals starve to death on our streets while others throw food away. It is the reason we have extra rooms in our homes while others sleep on the concrete at night in the winter. It is the reason we use technological advances—iPhones, video games, television, and other technologies—to waste time, moving closer to death, and distract us from our inner being. Sadly, these ways of journeying through the human experience are so common to us that we perceive them as normal.

It takes an individual that is wholeheartedly aligned with their higher self—the Universe within—to realize how filled with self-hatred the world has become. A world where more energy is wasted bringing each other down rather than picking each other up. A world where fights are cheered on and recorded rather than broken up. A world where individuals being bullied are laughed at rather than stood up for. These ways of being only occur due to individuals not seeing the love already manifested within them that will show how interconnected we all are despite our physical differences and societal labels.

The only way to find freedom in a world full of self-hatred is to cherish our individuality and love who we are. We perceive ourself as the individual we see in the mirror or on our front camera when we take a selfie, but these depictions do not represent who we are. We are not our body; we are what is within our body. We are what the human eye cannot see. When we believe that we are a body, we live life constantly thinking that something is lacking. We seek love external of our being—approval, attention, and belonging—instead of realizing that our being is love itself. Everything we need is already manifested within each of us; there is nothing lacking. The realization of this will free us from the unconscious state of self-hatred the world is full of and allow us to love ourself unconditionally.

Self-love is the answer to all of the problems in the world. With self-love, we will not hurt ourself or anyone else. There will be no gangs, no fights, no terrorists, no war, and no homelessness. Each individual will become joyously and intimately engaged with the

Universe and each other, perceiving everything as art. The human experience will become our playground of curiosity rather than something that causes us to live in fear, trapped in our comfort zone.

Love Yourself First

"I LOVE ME. I LOVE ME ENOUGH FOR THE BOTH OF US"

— *JHENÉ AIKO*

There is a verse in the Bible that states, "Love your neighbor as you love yourself." This Bible verse tells us that we must love ourself before we can love someone else, and before someone else can love us. It is the love we have for ourself that is equivalent to the amount of love we can give to others and receive from others. All of our bonds and relationships can only be equal to the loving foundation we have within, beyond our physical bodies.

Most of us get so caught up in searching for the perfect companion that we do not realize we are our own perfect companion. There is no individual on this Earth that has the power to love us like we can love ourself. Our conditioned mind has created this illusionary idea that love is something outside of our being, but truthfully, love can only be found by going within. By going within, we will cease to rely on external fulfillment and become happy with who we are in each moment.

Finding happiness with who we are in each moment and becoming self-reliant—not needing external fulfillment—gives us the ability to experience unconditional love. Most of us see self-reliance from a negative perspective. An individual that is self-reliant is perceived as lonely or abandoned, but this is a distorted way of thinking. Self-reliant individuals understand that in life they are on their own and have to love who they are before anyone else can see the love in them. They understand that even though they may want a relationship, it is not a necessity to have a relationship. Nevertheless, when a self-reliant individual does decide to get involved in a relationship, they are never dependent on their partner for love, attention, and happiness.

Most of us lack self-reliance and feel the need to rely on external subjects for love, attention, and happiness. We find it easier to push our problems onto other individuals and use the attention we receive from them as a tool to ignore our problems; not realizing that this way of journeying is a temporary solution. Receiving assistance from others for our problems due to the lack of love we have for ourself will never help us feel better about who we are; it only worsens our problems in the long run.

When we journey through the human experience without acknowledging our problems, we become accustomed to getting in relationships with wrong intentions. The fear of loneliness, the need for sex, physical attraction, as well as the need to impress our peers are all wrong reasons to get involved in a relationship. These wrong reasons lead us into horrible relationships, pushing us further away from loving ourself and cherishing our individuality.

Being in a relationship is not about becoming complete or happy. A healthy, strong, and trusting relationship can only transpire by entering the relationship already complete and happy with who we are. By entering a relationship already complete and happy with who we are, our relationship will not reflect a dependency on someone else, but instead reflect the power of togetherness. Depending on someone else derives from a deep, internal insecurity, directly reflecting a lack of self-love.

When we are insecure, we cannot learn to value others and ourself at the same time. We become accustomed to judging others, unconscious of knowing that each judgment reflects a judgment of ourself. Accepting the positive aspects and strengths of others becomes impossible because we prefer focusing on the weaknesses and flaws in others. Until we release our insecurities and love the wholeness of who we are, we will not have the ability to align with other souls and the Universe within our being.

Aligning with other souls and the Universe within allows us to stop seeking love in relationships with other individuals and start to find love in spiritual partnerships—individuals coming together for the purpose of spiritual growth. Relationships—having a boyfriend or girlfriend, husband or wife—are not the purpose of our journey through the human experience.

Our soul has manifested in a physical body for the purpose of interacting with other souls more intimately and finding spiritual partners. Spiritual partnerships not only bring a loving partner into our life, they also make the world a more loving place where self-hatred is nonexistent and each individual is accepted for who they are.

When we form spiritual partnerships, we recognize the existence of the Universe within each individual and make conscious choices to further its evolution. We live by values, perceptions, thoughts, and actions that commit to the spiritual growth of each individual soul. We no longer see lust as our primary purpose of bonding with individuals of the opposite sex, but instead, see spiritual growth as the primary purpose of bonding with individuals of the opposite sex. Each established spiritual partnership inspires us to fulfill our life purpose. This is the beauty of spiritual partnerships, an essential aspect of self-love.

The Parallel Of Self-Love And Power

"WHEN THE POWER OF LOVE OVERCOMES THE LOVE OF POWER, THE WORLD WILL KNOW PEACE."

— JIMI HENDRIX

In our society, power is perceived as having the ability to put forth strengths upon other individuals and take advantage of them. However, self-love is nonexistent in this kind of power. This type of power changes as time changes; therefore, it cannot be an accurate representation. Having muscles that can be used to intimidate others is a false representation of power. Physical beauty that can be used to influence others is a false representation of power. The ability to control others by having a lot of money is a false representation of power. All of these things change as time changes.

The mind, heart, and soul of the individual is where true power resides. We lack power when we place our mind, heart, and soul upon things such as money, cars, clothes, physical appearance, and other forms of perceived societal dominance. We acquire power when we place our mind, heart, and soul upon things such as compassion, truth, honesty, wisdom, and forgiveness. These ways of being align us with the Universe within and raise our individual level of vibrational frequency.

Power is the vibrational energy that resides deep, inside each of us. By living life from a state of self-love, we activate this power into our life and become guided toward nirvana—a state of bliss and peace. Living life from a state of self-love also inspires us to guide others toward nirvana, understanding the constant collaboration of energy between each soul sharing the human experience.

Instead of becoming a static energy system that hoards energy, we become a static energy system that lives a life of conscious acts filled with positivity. We release energy of love, gratitude, appreciation, care, and enlightenment. As a result, we become a magnet for positivity and those that want to become positive individuals. This is how the world becomes a better place simply by each individual soul loving who they are and finding the power within rather than seeking power external of their being.

Truthfully, there is no such thing as external power; it is an illusion that we perceive as real through societal labeling. Becoming overly consumed by the external world and the illusions it portrays to our mind causes our being to live in separation. We become separated from our individuality, higher consciousness, as well as the love we have for our true self—the individual we are within and placed on this Earth to be.

The need for external power is what led the Nazis to ruin the lives of six million Jews. It led James Earl Ray to kill Martin Luther King and Lee Harvey Oswald to kill John F. Kennedy. It set David against Goliath and the family of Romeo against the family of Juliet. There is never a positive outcome when an individual feels the need to acquire power external of his or her being.

Every individual that seeks to acquire power external of their being does not feel the love flowing within them, beyond their physical body. Instead of viewing the world as a learning environment, these individuals view the world as a competitive game. A game that perceives the winner as the individual that has acquired the most externals—money, sneakers, cars, houses, and other material possessions. However, any individual playing this game can never win because they are unconscious to the truth of their existence, which is to come into the physical world to see equality. Participating in this illusionary game is the reason billions of individuals have been stuck on Earth for many lifetimes instead of ascending to higher dimensions.

When we participate in this illusionary game, we perceive the individual driving a BMW as better than the individual driving a Honda. We perceive the boss as better than the employee. We perceive the celebrity as better than the homeless. We perceive the individual with a college degree as better than the individual without a college degree. We perceive the illusions presented to our mind as real rather than a diverse amount of vibrational frequencies.

Self-love gives us power over the external illusions rather than letting them have power over us. It gives us the higher consciousness of knowing that life itself is an illusion that allows us to interact with other souls in a more intimate manner. With self-love, we will understand that our sole purpose is to remain aligned with the Universe beyond our physical body and love who we are as an individual soul. Aligning with the Universe beyond our physical body and loving who we are as an individual soul is what makes us truly powerful and allows us to pass the test of this physical dimension, Earth.

How To Love Yourself

1. SPIRITUAL GROWTH

When we spend time growing spiritually, loving ourself becomes automatic. We become more peaceful, kind, loving, and compassionate, learning to nurture our mind as it grows more captivating each day.

2. LOOK BEYOND MATERIAL OBJECTS AND THE FEELING THEY BRING

There's a quote that states, "The person wearing the cloth should never love the cloth more than the person wearing it." This quote expresses the importance of loving ourself and not what we have. We all want nice houses, cars, clothes, and tons of money, but these externals should not influence the love we have for our being. Material possessions are temporary fixes.

3. HAVE FUN

It is essential that we have fun as we journey through the human experience; the human experience is meant to be enjoyable. Once we start to have fun and enjoy life, we will relax, embrace ourself, and quit worrying about things that do not matter.

4. TREAT OTHERS WITH KINDNESS

Bringing acts of love and kindness into the lives of others greatly contributes to the love we have for ourself. The smiles, thank-yous, hugs, and love we receive back from the acts of kindness we give out will naturally make us feel better about who we are.

Affirmations

1. I love myself unconditionally and accept myself as I am.

2. I accept myself for who I am and I am constantly trying to better myself.

3. I am worthy and so is everybody else. I love all.

4. I love myself and I love the world. I know that love is everything.

5. I am own best friend. I am also a friend to the world.

GOD GAVE YOU THEM SHOES TO FIT YOU, SO PUT THEM ON AND WEAR THEM. BE YOURSELF MAN, BE PROUD OF WHO YOU ARE. EVEN IF IT SOUNDS CORNY, DON'T LET NO ONE TELL YOU, YOU AIN'T BEAUTIFUL.

- EMINEM

Self-Perception Is Everything

"What you think of yourself is much more important than what others think of you."
— *Seneca*

IT DOES NOT MATTER how much makeup we put on before we go out, how well dressed we are at the bar, or how much money we have in our wallet if the perception we have of ourself is negative. We have all heard the quote, "Perception is everything." Truthfully, self-perception is everything. Self-perception is our belief of personal relevance in the world. The level of confidence we have in our ability to think for ourself, cope with disappointment, and chase our dreams depend upon our self-perception. Without a positive self-perception, our journey through the human experience will be miserable, causing us to constantly feel as if we are not good enough.

We have to move away from solely perceiving the world with our eyes and understand that we are all the same within, existing for a definite purpose. Regardless if we are the most intelligent or the least intelligent, the fattest or the skinniest, the most attractive or the least attractive, we have to know in our hearts who we are beyond these extrinsic masks. These extrinsic masks are representations of societal labels, and no societal label can ever define the beauty of our being. The more we seek stability in the external world, the more unstable our lives will become. True stability is only acquired by embracing our inner being and living through our Higher Self.

Our Higher Self represents the individual we are within and who we came into the physical world to be. When we are born, we have no sense of identity, consciously grasping the concept of unity. However, after experiencing the physical world and its pre-established rules of illusion, we start to believe that we have an identity. Our names, faces, families, thoughts, and beliefs start to consume our mind, causing us to develop a self-perception.

SELF-PERCEPTION IS EVERYTHING

Over time, our self-perception becomes a fundamental human need, controlling the way we experience life a part of the society. Everything we portray to the external world, from our thoughts, emotions, actions, beliefs, and intentions directly reflect our self-perception. Realism, intuitiveness, creativity, independence, ability to deal with change, and willingness to admit our mistakes represent qualities of an individual that has a positive self-perception. Blindness to reality, conformity, dependency, hostility toward others, and fear of change are ways of being that represent an individual that has a negative self-perception. A positive self-perception allows us to think, act, and relate to the world in a positive manner. In contrast, a negative self-perception allows us to think, act, and relate to the world in a negative manner. Either way, there is no hiding the way we perceive ourself; our self-perception is constantly dwelling inside our being, portraying a reflection to the external world.

Both internal and external subjects shape our self-perception. Internal subjects reside within; subjects such as our thoughts, beliefs, intentions, and behaviors.

External subjects consist of subjects in the environment; subjects such as teachers, parents, television, music, and social class. Despite our self-perception in the present moment, we should never doubt our ability to change the way we perceive ourself.

Factors During Our Childhood That Create A Negative Self-Perception

"A CHILD'S LIFE IS LIKE A PIECE OF PAPER ON WHICH EVERY PERSON LEAVES A MARK."

— CHINESE PROVERB

Although the construction of our self-perception is a lifelong process, the foundation of the way we perceive ourself is established during our childhood. During our childhood, our minds are extremely receptive and lack the ability to distinguish between the correct and incorrect ways to go about doing things. As a result, we become completely dependent on our parents. If the way our parents raise us is effective, we grow up to be an individual with a positive self-perception, journeying through the human experience in a positive and prosperous manner. However, if the way our parents raise us is ineffective, we grow up to be an individual with a negative self-perception, journeying through the human experience in a negative and scarce manner. Regardless if the way we were raised was a positive or negative experience, we can go beyond our parent's limitations in life as well as the limitations they place upon us.

Below are factors in our childhood that lead to the establishment of a negative self-perception. By gaining awareness to these factors, we activate the power within our being to change our life and the way we perceive ourself. It will allow us to let go of our emotional scars and understand that the past does not have to control the manifestations of our future.

PHYSICAL ABUSE

We may exhibit a negative self-perception if we were exposed to some form of physical abuse during our childhood. Physical abuse causes psychological disturbances and negative social skills, causing us to accept a life of being used and belittled.

Experiencing physical abuse in our childhood is an experience that most of us do not feel comfortable sharing with others, causing the experiences to become deeply rooted inside of our being for the rest of our life. We start to live life easily misled, taken advantage of, and feel undeserving of the finer things the world has to offer. Most of us that have been physically abused are aware of what we have endured in the past, but unaware of how damaged we could be from the experiences.

CRITICISM

During our childhood, we take everything our parents say to us as the truth because we have not yet established the ability to analyze the world and think for ourself. This is dangerous psychologically because the more negative our parents are to us, the more negative our self-perception becomes. We unconsciously internalize everything our parents say, causing the criticism we receive from them to become a part of who we are as an individual.

Criticism is often made when our parents are angry, hostile, and upset. Usually, it is because they are reminded of an experience in their life, representing an area of weakness, failure, or fear. Instead of our parents admitting this to themselves, they project their weaknesses, failures, and fears onto us in the form of belittling remarks. Truly, our parents are not criticizing us but reflecting on their past experiences and mental limitations.

NEGLIGENCE

When we are children, our observation skills overshadow our communication skills, causing us to cling to our parents and take on their ways. We cling to our parents in search for love and affection, which gives us a sense of emotional support. When we do not receive emotional support from our parents, we tend to feel extremely neglected, eventually crushing our self-perception.

Neglect gives off the impression that our emotions are unacceptable and do not matter. We push our feelings away with the intention of not bothering the outer world or ourself. Yet, pushing our feelings away can get us through our childhood without any problems, but as we grow older, they cause punishing self-perception issues.

BEING COMPARED TO OTHERS

It is common for our parents to compare us to others regardless if it is one of our cousins, a classmate, or a child portrayed on the television. There is nothing wrong with comparing, but when our parents compare without showing appreciation, our sense of individuality and positive self-perception diminishes. It gives us the impression that we have to make our parents proud and motivates us to be like the people our parents praise. Instead of cherishing our individuality we end up chasing the individuality of others, unintentionally living life under the mask of someone else, clueless to our own potential and beauty.

Societal Factors And Self-Perception

"WHEN YOU'RE SURROUNDED BY ALL THESE PEOPLE, IT CAN BE LONELIER THAN WHEN YOU'RE BY YOURSELF. YOU CAN BE IN A HUGE CROWD, BUT IF YOU DON'T FEEL LIKE YOU CAN TRUST ANYONE OR TALK TO ANYBODY, YOU FEEL LIKE YOU'RE REALLY ALONE."

— FIONA APPLE

EDUCATIONAL SYSTEM

The sole purpose of school is to morph us into good citizens, not better individuals. It does not encourage independence or independent thinking. It encourages us to memorize a shared body of knowledge, learn obedience to authority, and consume the rules of society. Most teachers demand obedience and conformity from their students by writing referrals to the principal, yelling, kicking students out of class, and calling parents. When teachers act in this manner, we start to unconsciously perceive ourself the way our teachers perceive and treat us, not as an individual, but as a part of the class.

SOCIAL MEDIA

The pressure of snapping the perfect selfie, with the perfect filter, wearing the perfect outfit has begun to dominate our lives. Most individuals believe that they are no more than social media likes, favorites, retweets, and followers. By investing huge amounts of time and effort into our digital identity, we develop an uncertainty of our individuality and a distorted self-perception.

We have to become the main provider to our self-perception and stop craving the approval of others via social media. Everyone's life will appear splendid from an outer perspective, but truthfully, we all have our individual struggles. Social media is one of the ways insecurities take control of our lives, and insecurity is what corporations and society as a whole thrive off of because it makes us feel as if we have to continuously invest in our outer self—buying clothes, shoes, cars, makeup, and other material possessions—rather than our internal self—thoughts, actions, intentions, emotions, behaviors, values, and beliefs.

TOXIC FRIENDS

A negative circle of influence also plays a vital role in the development of our self-perception. Sometimes we care for the individuals in our life so much that we become blinded by the ways they could be damaging us physically, mentally, and emotionally. It is imperative that we keep our circles of influence full of positivity; this includes individuals that believe in us, do not take us for granted, and encourage our spiritual growth.

Friends who poison our lives with negativity and drain our potential energy are considered "toxic" individuals. They tend to focus on controlling our life and disregard our needs and feelings. They perceive everyone in their life as a tool instead of beautiful, equal beings. It is hard to grasp the thought of anyone putting up with the actions of toxic individuals, but it is rather common as most individuals in our society lack self-love and a positive self-perception.

Every day we have to analyze our life as well as the individuals a part of our life. We have to distance ourself from any individual that generates feelings of unhappiness, unworthiness, and self-doubt. Life is too short to waste energy on those that do not deserve our energy.

CELEBRITIES AND HOLLYWOOD

In today's society, we are more likely to admire celebrities rather than our parents. We are subconsciously led to think money will make us happy and what we have is never enough. Human potential is being destroyed individual by individual because we are programmed to think we are less than those conveyed to us through the television screen, magazine ads, the Internet, and other glorified societal outlets.

Our minds are constantly fed programming that makes us think we are not good enough, skinny enough, or rich enough. The trends and images portrayed in the mainstream are unrealistic and tiresome to keep up with. For this reason, we must learn to be content with who we are and ignore the things we see as trendy and popular. Celebrities are placed in front of us to keep the capitalist economy going, instilling insecurity and self-hatred into the masses.

How To Improve Self-Perception

1. BE TRUE TO YOURSELF

Being true to who we are is the best thing we can do to improve our self-perception. Sometimes we put an excessive amount of energy into pleasing others and forget the importance of self. We have to move away from this unconscious habit of pleasing others and realize we are responsible for our own happiness, not the happiness of others.

2. ALLOW YOURSELF TO BE WHERE YOU ARE

At times, we become so consumed by thoughts of the future or remain stuck in the past that we become miserable in the present moment. The present moment is the only thing we have control over and can enjoy to the fullest. The next second of our life is never promised, so we have to live for the beauty of each moment and accept ourself for who we are in each moment.

3. BE GRATEFUL

When we become grateful, we start to perceive the world differently. We begin to see the positive aspects of everything and everyone. Before we go to bed each night, we need to write down ten things we are grateful for as well as the reasons we are grateful them. It is gratitude alone that has the power to change our life and the way we perceive ourself.

4. INDIVIDUALIZE COMPLIMENTS

To individualize compliments means to accept and embrace each compliment we receive, not only the ones we agree with but also the compliments we disagree with. When other individuals give us a compliment or suggestion we do not agree with, we should be inspired to keep bettering ourself.

Affirmations

1. I am created to be unique.

2. I accept myself for who I am.

3. I am worthy of everything that I desire.

4. I deserve to have a great life.

5. I am beautiful both internally and externally.

"A BEAUTIFUL PERSON IS NOT DEFINED BY A HAIR STYLE, A PAIR OF SHOES, IT'S NOT THE LOGOS ON THE T-SHIRT, THE SPORT'S TEAM ON A HAT, THE DESIGNER'S NAME ON A HAND BAG, OR EVEN HOW YOU SMELL.

INSTEAD, BEAUTY LIES IN WHO YOU ARE WHEN NO ONE IS WATCHING, THE PERSON YOU ARE WHEN THERE'S NOTHING TO HIDE BEHIND. NO AMOUNT OF CONCEALER CAN COVER UP A CANTANKEROUS HEART, BUT ALL THE MAKE-UP IN THE WORLD CAN'T ADD A SINGLE LUMEN TO THE BRIGHTNESS OF A BEAUTIFUL SOUL."

— JUSTIN YOUNG

Don't Doubt You (Self-Doubt)

"The worst enemy to creativity is self-doubt."
— *Sylvia Plath*

In this era of technology, fast media, and popular trends we are under an abundant amount of external pressures that challenge our ability to think for ourself. Many of us have adopted the norms pre-established by our family and society, causing us to blindly accept life for what it is and never question what appears to be normal. This neglects our free will and natural birth right of forming our own opinions, making us a robot to someone else's mental programming, falling victim to blind conformity.

Blind conformity, much like self-hatred, is the essence of all suffering and regret in the world. Many wars have started because the general public placed their blind faith in corrupt leaders. Slavery, racism, discrimination toward women, and religious extremism—individuals that believe anyone that does not agree with their religion is evil and flawed—all stem from blind conformity.

During the Cold War, in the 1950s, blind conformity became normal to American citizens. The rise of television programming that instilled societal norms into viewers were broadcasted in nearly every household, giving individuals a sense of how they should look, how they should act, and how they should think. People were urged to go to church, to be patriotic, to work hard, and to raise their families without questioning if they truly wanted to do these things. Men and women were programmed to perceive getting married and having a family as the supreme accomplishment as an adult, causing individuals to get married younger than we do in present day, neglecting their individual goals and dreams. The individuals that were awakened to the abundant amount of conformity taking place in the American society felt the need to remain conformed, living life from a state of self-doubt.

Self-doubt is an illusion of the mind that serves as a form of mental slavery. It encloses us within a limited range of action, ultimately hindering our growth. The more we doubt ourself, the less power we have and the less prosperous our life becomes. Most individuals doubt themselves into a life of scarcity, negativity, and denial to reality, the worst way of abandoning our individuality.

By abandoning our individuality through self-doubt, we live life from a state of fear, falling victim to the illusions of the external world. All forms of fear, including self-doubt, are human emotions that have been implanted in our mind since early infancy. We were not born thinking, "I can do this" or "I cannot do that," these are thoughts that have derived from the conditioning of society and those we have come in contact with on our journey through the human experience. Truthfully, there is nothing we cannot do; it is only our mind that limits us.

Self-doubt may appear to be a psychological issue, but it is not; it is an emotion that can be controlled by educating and shifting our mindset. We have to learn that self-doubt is not an emotion intended to hold us back, but an emotion intended to push us forward. Once we reeducate our mind and see self-doubt from a more realistic perspective, we will see the world as a less threatening and more joyous environment, embracing the beautiful experiences of life without labeling them as good or bad.

Most of us doubt ourself because we believe that we cannot handle the unfamiliar situation life will present to us once we go beyond our comfort zone. Truthfully, our being is so powerful that there is no situation we cannot handle. We can handle any situation we experience by having a positive perception of the experience and not attempting to control the world beyond our being. We cannot control the actions of our employer, our significant other, our close friends, or what makes the headline news. The only thing we can control is our perception and have the ability to see the light in each situation.

Unfamiliar situations will always bring the burden of self-doubt into our life. However, instead of being defeated by the doubt we place upon ourself, we must ask, "How is it possible for me to move forward in life if I think negatively about expanding beyond my comfort zone?" When we do the same routine things and fear attempting something different it becomes impossible for us to progress. Instead of questioning whether or not the grass is greener on the other side, we have to learn to trust our vibrations enough to take the chance and cherish the experience. Even the Bible says, "Walk by faith and not by sight."

When we repeatedly tell ourself that we cannot do something, we will never do it. We will never think big, have the strength to open our mind, or fulfill our life purpose. Our life will turn into a life of idolizing celebrities, unaware of the fact that they are born into the world with the same human anatomy as everyone else in the society. The only difference between the celebrities we idolize and ourself is their ability to act upon self-doubt, allowing them to go beyond the norm and stand out.

Having the courage to take risks and see the light in each situation in hopes of a potential reward is what makes individuals such as Mark Zuckenberg, Warren Buffett, Steve Jobs, and Oprah Winfrey successful, not their material abundance. Imagine if every human being that has ever walked the face of the Earth let self-doubt take control of their life. There would be no such thing as houses, cars, television, Instagram, or the iPhone. Believing in ourself is the only way we can express our individuality to the world and have the confidence to fulfill our life purpose.

Misunderstanding of Failure

"I HAVE NOT FAILED. I'VE JUST FOUND 10,000 WAYS THAT WON'T WORK."

— *THOMAS EDISON*

Our misunderstanding of failure greatly impacts the various ways we doubt ourself. We perceive individuals that are homeless, in jail, or poor as failures, subconsciously causing us to fear taking risks and go beyond the status quo. However, no situation of homelessness, imprisonment, or being poor can establish an individual as a failure. No societal factor or label represents failure. Failure is the best thing that can happen in our life; it is our distorted perception that makes it appear to be a horrible thing.

The difference between individuals that live a prosperous life and individuals that live an average life resides in their perception of failure. Individuals that live an average life perceive failure as a bad thing, mostly due to the conditioning of their mind through the formal education system. On the contrary, individuals that live a prosperous life understand that failure births success. Every genius and successful individual that has ever walked the face of the Earth is someone that has failed an abundant amount of times but never perceived himself or herself as a failure.

The television screen, magazines, and the Internet do not show the mistreatment, hard work, trials, and tribulations the perceived successful individuals had to endure on their journey to success. This causes us to believe that these individuals never experienced failure rather than understanding that failure is what contributed to their success. Michael Jordan, said to be the greatest basketball player ever, was cut from his high school basketball team and told he was not good enough. The Ford Motor Company was Henry Ford's third business following his first two that did not see success. Walt Disney, the pioneer of cartoon films and creator of Disneyland, was fired by the editor of a newspaper for lacking creative ideas. Albert Einstein, the world's greatest scientist, was told he would "never amount to anything" when he was younger because he could not speak until a late age and failed in school. Thomas Edison, the inventor of electricity, motion pictures, and the kinetophone, was told as a child that he was too dumb to learn anything. These individuals along with many others that achieved success never saw themselves as a failure no matter how many times they failed. They let their failures inspire them to keep trying, eventually mastering their craft.

Eighty-five percent of small businesses in the United States fail within the first two years. That means eighty-five out of every one hundred small business ventures fail within its first two years. Depending on how passionate the particular entrepreneur is, he or she either stops trying to bring their business plan to light or understands that failure is a part of the process. The richest man in the world, Warren Buffett, even says he would not invest in any business where the owner of the business has not failed at least twice. Mr. Buffett understands that it takes failure to succeed.

No matter how many times we fail on our journey through the human experience, we must develop the strength to keep trying. It is our willingness to keep trying that makes us a potential success. Failure is the secret to success; however, most individuals in our society cannot grasp this concept and decide to hold themselves back from being judged by others for their failures. Failure is to be embraced, not frowned upon.

Opinions of External Sources

"CONFORMITY IS THE JAILER OF FREEDOM AND THE ENEMY OF GROWTH."

— JOHN F. KENNEDY

Once we realize that we do not have to journey through the human experience following the paths of others or what appears to be the norm, our life will become more prosperous, blessed, and blissful. The only way to experience bliss is to cherish our individuality, align with the Universe within, and stop caring about the opinions of external sources. By caring about the opinions of external sources, we are repressed from living life the way we desire, bringing the burden of self-doubt in everything we plan to do.

We waste a vast amount of time and energy on subjects that do not deserve our time and energy. We ask ourself questions such as, "How am I perceived? What do they think about me? How does my life appear from the perception of others?" These are questions of self-doubt that dominate our life and keep us from expressing the fullness of our individuality. When we let go of these destructive ways of thinking and stop caring what other individuals think of us, we will free ourself from the illusion of right and wrong and live freely through our experiences.

Freeing ourself from the illusion of right and wrong and living freely through our experiences allows us to have confidence in our thoughts, actions, ideas, visions, and goals. It is a freedom that allows us to believe in ourself and put time and effort into things we are passionate about. The only way to completely free ourself is to rely solely on our own ways of thinking and make decisions without seeking acceptance from external sources. The more we doubt our own judgment and care what other individuals think, the more we are robbing the world of our full potential.

The Wright Brothers were labeled as "crazy" when they believed that they could build an aircraft and fly across the ocean. Mark Zuckenberg was labeled as "crazy" when he decided to dropout of college because he believed in his appeared to be corny Facebook idea. Socrates was labeled as "crazy," imprisoned, and put to death by the Athenian democracy for urging others to think for themselves. Jesus, the ancient spiritual philosopher, was labeled as "crazy" and crucified because he wanted more individuals to see the powers of I AM—the powers of God that exist within each of us. Neither of these individuals cared about the opinions of those external of their being, and relied solely on their individual ways of thinking.

There is no need to waste our time and energy trying to convince others of our point of view. We are not born into the world to live up to the expectations of others. We are born into the world to express the fullness of our individuality. To express the fullness of our individuality, we have to free ourself from the mental enslavement of caring what other individuals think.

Overcoming Self-Doubt

1. KEEP TRYING

Self-doubt never goes away, we just get better at dealing with it over time. Every time we attempt to go beyond our comfort zone we will experience self-doubt. The key is in not becoming defeated by the doubt we place upon ourself and continuing to take the risk.

2. JUST BELIEVE

We should never reach a point in our life where we believe we are not good enough. No matter what the circumstance is, we are never making it better by not believing in ourself. Truthfully, there is nothing in the Universe we cannot conquer by utilizing the power of desire, faith, and action.

3. FIND THE WORST-CASE SCENARIO

Before we become defeated by self-doubt, we must weigh out the worst thing that can happen if we take the chance and fail. We should think, "What's the worst that could happen?" and prepare for that outcome. Exploring the possibility of everything that could go wrong makes us feel safer and more prepared to take the chance.

Affirmations

1. My self-doubt is natural. It does not define me.

2. Perfection is an illusion that I will not chase.

3. I believe in myself.

4. I am capable of living a life beyond my wildest dreams.

DON'T DOUBT YOU

"By fully experiencing and going beyond an emotional block - through the layers of doubt and fear - you experience the emotion of who you truly are."

— Stephen Richards

What Aretha Franklin Really Meant (Self-Respect)

"When you are content to be simply yourself and don't compare or compete, everyone will respect you." — Lau Tzu

THE LEGENDARY ARETHA FRANKLIN SAID IT best, "R-E-S-P-E-C-T." **Respect. Respect. Respect.** Respect is a combination of appreciation, admiration, and recognition. To respect someone means to value, honor, and accept them for who they are regardless the color of their skin, monetary value, or personal belief system. In the most simplistic explanation, it is treating other individuals the same way we want to be treated.

Like many things, respect begins with self. We have to respect ourself to the core for other individuals to respect us. The less respect we have for ourself, the less other individuals will respect us. Lack of self-respect is reflected in our thoughts, emotions, actions, and beliefs, giving other individuals in this competitive world the sense to take advantage of our being. On the contrary, the more we respect ourself, the more other individuals will respect us and treat us of equal value. All in all, we cannot demand respect from others if we do not respect ourself.

Self-respect is the most priceless asset we can acquire in a world that has become so selfish and greedy. It allows us to live life from a state of inner peace and harmony rather than living life from a state of self-denial, doing anything, even if we are unhappy, for money. It allows us to cherish our individuality and not conform to the world beyond our being, even if we feel like an outcast. With self-respect, being unhappy due to the external dynamics of other individuals and the society is impossible.

The foundation of self-respect is in understanding that we were born into the physical world to be unique, outstanding, and cherish who we are within. It means being conscious to the fact that we are equal to every other entity on this planet; just as deserving of respect, success, happiness, love, and appreciation as the people we waste time and energy idolizing on the television screens, concerts, magazines, and the Internet. Most individuals in our society lack self-respect, therefore, they turn to celebrities to admire the lives that they have and the things they have accomplished. Once we establish a foundation of self-respect, we will stop wasting our time idolizing celebrities and work towards building a legacy of our own.

Most of us have a difficult time respecting ourself because we continuously look to other individuals for permission to feel of equal value and deserving of respect, success, happiness, love, and appreciation. Truthfully, our existence should be enough for us to feel deserving of respect, success, happiness, love, and appreciation; not every soul in the non-physical world has the honor of experiencing life in a more intimate manner. It means that we are here, on Earth, for a definite purpose. Once we stop looking outside ourself for a feeling of deservedness and realize we are a spiritual being, full of light, and have the powers of the Creator manifested within our physical body, we will develop a foundation of self-respect.

Sometimes our ability to respect ourself will make other individuals outraged, irritated, and sad, but it is only because these individuals want to dictate our actions, subconsciously believing that we are responsible for their happiness. Regardless of how they feel about whatever is being experienced, it is only right to stay true to ourself, aligned with the Universe within. As time passes, the individual will see their accountability in the situation and apologize for their reaction to us simply respecting our being. However, if the individual does not see their accountability in the situation or apologize for their reaction to us simply respecting our being, it means they are toxic and do not deserve to be in our life.

Before we gain self-respect, we have to know who we are beyond the labels society place upon us—black, white, rich, poor, beautiful, ugly, smart, dumb, and other illusionary labels. We have to know what we stand for, what we believe, what our priorities are, and the type of person we desire to become in the future. By knowing these subjects, it becomes easier to respect ourself and set boundaries for those external of our being. For instance, if we believe that we deserve nothing but the best in our relationships, then we will not allow anyone to do us wrong. If our significant other cheats on us, we will forgive them, but no longer associate with their being. If we find out our closest friends are talking behind our back, we will forgive them, but no longer associate with their being. Self-respect is the key to maintaining a high level of happiness, balance, and success on our journey through the human experience.

Beliefs

"BE SURE YOU PUT YOUR FEET IN THE RIGHT PLACE, THEN STAND FIRM."

— ABRAHAM LINCOLN

Our beliefs are the individual laws that delegate our journey through the human experience. Because of our beliefs each of us is living a different reality, experiencing life completely different than each other. For this reason, we must start living life from a perspective of, "his or her beliefs are not my beliefs, and my beliefs are not his or her beliefs." Once we journey through the human experience with this perspective, we will subconsciously respect each other, realizing that we all have our own personal model of reality.

What is reality?

The clearest explanation of reality would be imagining three men at the beginning of human existence encountering a **giraffe**. The first man tells the other two men that the **giraffe** is a bird. The second man tells the other two men that the **giraffe** is a lion. The third man tells the other two men that the **giraffe** is an oak tree.

If this is the case, which of the three men are correct?

All three of the men are correct because they each have a different belief of what a **giraffe** is. Reality is not about what is right and what is wrong; it has everything to do with our individual beliefs about what is right and what is wrong.

Truly, we have no idea what is going on in life so to say what is right and what is wrong is ignorant. Most individuals pretend to know what is going in life by following the beliefs and trends that are popular, but beyond the illusions they use to distract themselves, they subconsciously realize that they have no idea what is going on in life. It would be much easier to love and respect each another if we let go of our egos and acknowledge that we have no idea what life is or what is going on in life. It is only our individual beliefs that interpret what is going on in life, but no belief can ever be right and no belief can ever be wrong.

Too many of us are egotistic about our beliefs and do not respect the beliefs of others. We are close-minded and believe that our beliefs are the only truth, but this way of reasoning is distorted, stemming from a stream of lower consciousness. The beautiful thing about our beliefs is that we can have whatever beliefs we choose to have. If someone chooses to believe in Christianity, that is fine. If someone does not choose to believe in Christianity, that is fine. If someone chooses to believe that cheerleading is a sport, that is fine. If someone chooses to believe that cheerleading is not a sport, that is fine. It is okay to believe whatever we want to believe, but we have to understand that nothing we believe is real; everything, with an exception to nature, comes to light from the human imagination.

An important part of cherishing our individuality and having self-respect is in grasping the concept of beliefs. The longer we journey through the human experience without understanding that everything we experience daily is a belief based upon our individual perception, and that truly there is no right or wrong way to perceive the physical world, the longer we will suffer as a species. By establishing our own beliefs and valuing the beliefs of others, each individual finds comfort in cherishing their individuality, allowing the physical world to become more blissful than the human mind can grasp in the present moment.

Peer Pressure

"I'M NOT IN THIS WORLD TO LIVE UP TO YOUR EXPECTATIONS AND YOU'RE NOT IN THIS WORLD TO LIVE UP TO MINE."

— *BRUCE LEE*

Peer pressure is another essential aspect of self-respect. Peer pressure consists of all the voices and opinions in the world beyond our being that bombard our ability to be who we are as an individual. Falling victim to peer pressure is extremely common no matter the age of our being. The first time most individuals do drugs is because of peer pressure. Most teens are peer pressured by society to think they have to go to college and get a degree to be successful although it may not work for them. Nine out of ten teenage females are peer pressured into having sex for the first time. These are all results of individuals lacking self-respect, falling victim to peer pressure.

Peer pressure is the powerful external force that sends our life in the opposite direction than what we intend. To overcome peer pressure, we have to be strong-willed and not let the fear of being shunned by others keep us from the things we truly desire and individually believe as right or wrong. We have to move away from the approach of listening to what other individuals think and learn to think for ourself. When we cannot think for ourself, we give others the power to think for us, leading us on a path of self-destruction.

Being surrounded with supportive, positive, and open-minded individuals is another approach to avoiding peer pressure; however, peer pressure cannot be fully avoided. According to Jim Rohn, we are the average of our five closest friends. The five people we hang around the most are a direct reflection of who we are in the present moment as well as who we will become in the future. If our five closest friends smoke cigarettes, then chances are we smoke cigarettes. If our five closest friends party every weekend, chances are we party every weekend. If our five closest friends are not goal-oriented and do not want a better life for themselves, chances are we are not goal-oriented and do not want a better life for ourself. Therefore, if we wish to make changes in our life, our friends will not understand and pull us into the face of peer pressure. The best thing we can do is distance ourself from them completely and form a new circle of influence.

We have reached a point in human existence where it has become challenging not to fall prey to peer pressure. Individuals bully, fight, and harass other individuals for standing up for themselves and not conforming to the pressure placed upon them. Without self-respect, we are most vulnerable to letting the opinions of others define who we are and become victimized by peer pressure. It is okay to be different; we are born to be unique. We should be applauded for cherishing our individuality and having self-respect, not bullied or peer pressured.

Developing Self-Respect

1. TAKE ON THE PROCESS OF GETTING TO KNOW YOURSELF

The more we understand and get to know ourself, the more we appreciate our uniqueness and respect our being. The process of discovering who we are—our values, beliefs, dominant thoughts, strengths, and weaknesses—will take a great amount of time, but the results will improve our life in magical ways.

2. BE CONFIDENT

If we are not confident in who we are, how we look, or the life we live it will become difficult for us to respect ourself. We have to sincerely respect our being and become confident in who we are before anyone else will do the same. Self-respect and confidence are what made Socrates, Plato, Anselm, Martin Luther King Jr., and other historic figures powerful, influential individuals. They demanded respect for their beliefs and had the confidence to openly express them with the world.

3. REMOVE ALL FORMS OF RESENTMENT AND JEALOUSY

To respect ourself we have to stop wishing we possessed what other individuals possess and understand we are created to have different talents, gifts, thoughts, beliefs, and accomplishments. Showing resentment and jealousy toward other individuals is to subconsciously wish to be someone we are not; the ultimate form of disrespect to our being. It is important that we remove and become conscious of every thought, emotion, intention, and action of jealousy to increase the respect we have for ourself.

4. STOP TRYING TO KEEP UP WITH OTHERS

Living up to our own standards and working to achieve the goals we want to achieve rather than living up to the expectations of others is an important aspect of self-respect. It is much more important to do what we enjoy doing rather than following the path everyone else prefers to follow or perceives as normal. Doing what we are passionate about is the only way to fulfill our inner being and find freedom in a world that glorifies conformity.

Affirmations

1. I treat others as I expect to be treated.
2. I always find the time to thank people for their kindness.
3. I always search for goodness in the people.
4. In respecting all living things, I respect myself.
5. I naturally attract respect because I respect myself.

"WE ARE ALL ALONE, BORN ALONE, DIE ALONE, AND—IN SPITE OF TRUE ROMANCE MAGAZINES—WE SHALL ALL SOMEDAY LOOK BACK ON OUR LIVES AND SEE THAT, IN SPITE OF OUR COMPANY, WE WERE ALONE THE WHOLE WAY. I DO NOT SAY LONELY—AT LEAST, NOT ALL THE TIME—BUT ESSENTIALLY, AND FINALLY, ALONE. THIS IS WHAT MAKES YOUR SELF-RESPECT SO IMPORTANT, AND I DON'T SEE HOW YOU CAN RESPECT YOURSELF IF YOU MUST LOOK IN THE HEARTS AND MINDS OF OTHERS FOR YOUR HAPPINESS."

— HUNTER S. THOMPSON

Never Stop Evolving (Self-Progression)

"I am always trying to be better than I am."

— Lil' Wayne

SELF-PROGRESSION REQUIRES US TO LEARN constantly and expand our knowledge. English Renaissance statesman and philosopher, Francis Bacon, said it best, "Knowledge is power." Knowledge prepares us to make educated decisions and can be applied to any situation we encounter. The knowledge we acquire through self-progression gives us the ability to accomplish anything we desire on our journey through the human experience.

Despite our present situation, we have to take control of our life by continuously progressing through our experiences. If we fail a class, it is our individual choice to either give up or retake the class and dedicate ourself to studying more the next semester. If we do not make the sports team at school, it is our individual choice to either give up on the sport or work harder at acquiring the skills to increase the chances of making the team next year. No matter what we experience, we have the choice to evolve or retreat, to take responsibility for our life or fall victim to external circumstances.

Most of us get in the habit of blaming external circumstances—parents, teachers, the government, and other sources beyond our inner being—for the way our life has manifested. However, everything that has manifested into our life has come into our physical reality due to the individual we have become. Excuses, complaining, and blame all derive from the mind of individuals that do not understand they have direct control over their life by further evolving their being. When we are not further evolving our being through the process of self-progression, we tend to fall victim to the external world, exposing ourself to subjects that distract us from the truth of our existence.

By neglecting to progress each and every day, we become stagnant and lose our excitement towards life; the excitement we have during our childhood. Once we lose our excitement for life, we settle for a life of unconscious self-hatred, complaining, and wasting a third of our day working under the reign of another human being. We become mentally enslaved by the ordering of society and work harder on our jobs than we do on ourself. Our primary focus becomes our survival through monetary gain rather than further evolving our being, a very destructive way of journeying through the human experience.

We all want to be successful, but the majority of us have a distorted perception of success. We view success as something we pursue instead of something we become. We view success as a monetary value rather than an emotion. We view success as something that only a select few obtain rather than something we work toward each and every day of our life. To have more success in life, we have to become more deserving of success through the process of self-progression.

Self-progression is a never-ending process; to not progress is equivalent to death. There should never be a point in our life where we feel there is no room for improvement because there is always something we can improve on. We all know those "use to be" individuals that talk about what they use to do or what they accomplished in the past. These are individuals that have stopped progressing and neglect their current realities instead of continuing to improve each and every day.

Discovering Your Gift

"THE MEANING OF LIFE IS TO FIND YOUR GIFT. THE PURPOSE OF LIFE IS TO GIVE IT AWAY."

— *PABLO PICASSO*

Most of us set our hearts solely upon graduating college, getting a job, and making someone else rich. We become so consumed by our daily routine of waking up to an alarm clock, spending eight hours at school or work, and coming home to relax that we lose awareness to our purpose of coming into the physical world. We forget that our purpose is not to serve man, but to live through our spiritual gift that the Creator manifested within each of us at birth.

The Creator of the Universe created each of us with a spiritual gift to share with the world. Our gift is the one thing we can do the best even if minimum effort is applied. It is unique and cannot be taken away from us by any external determinant. It is what will lead us to a life of bliss, inner peace, and financial prosperity.

To add value to the world, we have to apply our spiritual gift. Becoming a professional athlete, being musically talented, or getting a high-paying job are not representations of individuals that have applied their spiritual gift. These are simply platforms for these individuals to share their spiritual gift with the world. When Kevin Durant received the MVP Award for the 2013-2014 NBA season, he stated, "I would like to thank God for changing my life and letting me realize what life is all about. Basketball is just a platform in order for me to inspire people and I realize that." Kevin Durant discovered that he was placed into the physical world with the gift of inspiring others, and he does that on the platform of being a professional basketball player.

Most of us have a hard time discovering our gift because we attach it to or define it as a job, but our job is not our gift. Our gift is something that can be applied to every aspect of our life—relationships, business, and community. It is something that is connected to us regardless if we are working or vacationing, with our friends or alone.

Steve Jobs, one of the greatest innovators to ever walk the face of the Earth, had a gift of seeing technology in a way that changed the world. He advanced technology in a way that revolutionized the human experience beyond the human imagination. Every time we enter an Apple Store or unlock our iPhones, it is because Steve Jobs recognized his gift and shared it with the world. The ability to innovate and transform technology was Steve Jobs' gift that he left on Earth after passing away. Imagine how different life would be if Steve Jobs neglected to discover his gift and mindlessly went through life following the norm.

By journeying through the human experience neglecting to discover and apply our gift, we will never feel fulfilled or reach a state of nirvana. Life in the physical dimension will be miserable rather than a Heaven on Earth experience. Our gift is the only thing we need to survive and prosper, however, the norms and conditioning of society blind us to the truth of having a gift.

Formal Education vs. Self Education

FORMAL EDUCATION WILL MAKE YOU A LIVING; SELF-EDUCATION WILL MAKE YOU A FORTUNE.

— JIM ROHN

There is more to learning than attending school. Whether we have a Ph.D. or a high school diploma, there is always something to learn each and every day of our life. Formal education is important with regards to the means of society, but the learning process should not be limited to a classroom.

On TED Talk in 2006, Ken Robinson affirmed, "Every day we attend school we become less intelligent."

How could this be possible if we go to school for the sole purpose of learning and accumulating knowledge? It is because the knowledge we acquire from school is for the benefit of society. The knowledge we receive from school does not contribute to the evolution of our being or establish us as intelligent. True intelligence has been manifested within each of us since birth.

Formal education makes us academically intelligent, which is the concept of intelligence defined and created by man. It diminishes our true, authentic intelligence that is manifested within our being by the Creator, which is our creative intelligence. It teaches us what to think rather than teaching us how to think. *It morphs us into good citizens, not better individuals.* It conditions our mind to think that without formal education we are worthless and limited to experiencing success in life.

True success is experiencing and living life from a constant state of happiness. There are engineers, doctors, lawyers, and teachers that society perceives as successful that do not feel successful because they are not happy. Truthfully, spending eight of the twenty-four hours of our day, five of our seven days a week, working under someone else's reign is not success, it is a roadblock to developing our creativity. Deep inside our being, we will always feel that we were placed on Earth for a higher purpose, yet, we fall victim to what society defines as success.

We cannot make a positive impact on the evolution of human existence by solely following what is viewed as the norm. Our purpose in life is to make an impact, not to work jobs that fail to expand our creativity and hinder our species from evolving. We have the power within to open our own doors. We have the power within to start our own companies. We have the power within to create whatever we desire; for everything starts in the form of a thought. Steve Jobs, Mark Zuckenberg, David Karp, and many other individuals have awakened to the powers within their being, using their creative intelligence to make a positive impact on the physical world.

The key to creating something of our own and boosting our creative intelligence can be found in the art of self-education. Jim Rohn, an American entrepreneur, author, and motivational speaker, preached to the world, "Formal education will make you a living. Self-education will make you a fortune." Fortune can be whatever we individually define it as. It can be our financial status, our happiness, our health, and even our physical appearance. Fortune is whatever we desire and value the most as an individual soul.

It is believed that since we are in school or finished with school that we are done learning. This is the most misunderstood concept by individuals in our society. We all need to continue learning, not just the skills needed for our job, major, or businesses, but most importantly learning about ourself. We need to learn about what makes us mad, what makes us happy, how we define success, and what motivates us to become better individuals. To continue learning, we have to become curious and fascinated with subjects we have no knowledge about. We are living in the Information Era; there is no excuse for us not being able to figure things out on our own. Information about everything that exist in the world or has once existed in the world can be found by researching. When we self-educate, we are both the teacher and the student.

Some individuals prefer to learn through trial and error, which is another form of self-education, but it is extremely easier for us to learn by picking up a book and reading. Reading allows us to learn from the experiences of others. How to raise kids, build relationships, find inner peace, and information about life hundreds of years ago can be found by reading a book. It is not about believing everything that we read; it is more about taking someone else's experience and being able to apply it to our own life.

Most people within our society claim that they are too busy to read, but the idea of "too busy" is an illusion in itself. One can always wake up thirty minutes earlier or go to sleep thirty minutes later; however, the words "too busy" are generally used as an excuse for a lack of priority. Individuals that neglect reading become robots to their culture, society, and close-minded to any other ways of thinking outside of the norm.

The Ancient Greeks understood the power of reading manuscripts and spent most of their time discussing ideas. When the great Greek scholars fled the city of Constantinople before the invasion of the Ottoman Turks, they brought all of their manuscripts into Europe. These manuscripts are the reason the Renaissance Era (1450-1600) was extremely popular and the most powerful era in all of human existence. The individuals a part of the Renaissance Era understood the power of making time to read and replacing wasted time with productivity. Idea after idea was brought to life every day during the Renaissance Era, simply because they understood the power of continually growing and educating themselves.

Keys To Self-Progression

1. KEEP POSITIVE THOUGHTS FLOWING

Thinking positive is the secret to every success story. Our mind has to believe that something can be done before the belief can manifest into physical reality. By becoming conscious of the thoughts inside our mind, we have the ability to take control of our life and allow progress. If we experience a negative thought, we must stop and replace the thought with a positive thought. As the Dalai Lama once stated, "The way to overcome negative thoughts and destructive emotions is to develop opposing, positive emotions that are stronger and more powerful."

2. LEARN A NEW SKILL EACH MONTH

Self-education is the key to living a healthy, prosperous, and blissful life. Self-education opens us up to a series of possibilities in the real world, making us a jack-of-all-trades. Being a jack-of-all-trades allows us to deal with life in a less problematic manner. In school, we learn about one skill and expect to use it all of our life to prosper, a major illusion.

3. WORSHIP CHANGE

Learning to worship change is essential to the level of happiness and success we obtain on our journey through the human experience. Most individuals go through life resisting change, keeping their lives from progressing. Without change, there is no progress; the two subjects work together.

4. SEE THE LIGHT IN EACH SITUATION

Everything that we experience on our journey is a lesson from the Creator to initiate progress. However, most of us let our experiences take control of us and play the victim. We focus on the negatives of each experience rather than the positives, causing us to settle, not improve.

Affirmations

1. I learn something new everyday.
2. Stepping outside of my comfort zone is necessary for growth.
3. If I want something I've never had, I must do something I've never done.
4. I determine the meaning and direction of my life.
5. I am dedicated to my passion in life.

"How noble and good everyone could be if, every evening before falling asleep, they were to recall to their minds the events of the whole day and consider exactly what has been good and bad. Then without realizing it, you try to improve yourself at the start of each new day."

— ANNE FRANK

PART II.

FOR HUMANITY: UNIVERSAL LAWS: ONENESS, VIBRATION, ATTRACTION

The Universe
(Laws)

"The discovery of natural law is a meeting with God. " — *Friedrich Dessauer*

WE OFTEN CONFUSE THE WORDS world and Universe, having no set definition for the two distinct interpretations of sound waves. We do not consciously realize that the Earth is a speck compared to the massive Universe. The world refers to human civilization and the planet that allows humanity to survive and prosper. For example, if human existence lived on Jupiter instead of Earth, we would refer to Jupiter as the world, not Earth. The Universe represents everything in existence—humanity, animals, plants, planets, the ocean, space, time (not the time of man-made clocks), matter, stars, gravity, and energy.

THE UNIVERSE (LAWS)

Just as there are laws that govern the world, there are laws that also govern the Universe. The laws that individuals are taught to abide by, only existing in the world, are Civil Laws. Civil Laws apply to subjects such as traffic lights, taxes, underage drinking, fraud, and country borders. However, the laws that govern the Universe, representing the mathematically advanced mind of the Creator, are Universal Laws. Universal Laws are the laws that elitist and leaders of the world attempt to keep away from the masses, intending to make us believe that we are powerless. According to ancient philosopher, Thomas Aquinas, Universal Law is the rational plan of God by which all creation is ordered.

Universal Law governs the Sun, the Moon, the weather, the ocean, the trees, and every other living entity. Everything in the Universe exists in perfect harmony with these laws. Over 5,000 years ago, in Ancient Egypt, Ancient Greece, and Ancient India, the Universal Laws were practiced, preached, and used to create prosperous civilizations. As human beings, we are given an individual consciousness for the purpose of mastering and abiding by these beautiful laws, giving us the ability to experience prosperity in every aspect of our lives.

Sadly, we have reached a point in human existence where the governing of Universal Law has become secondary, and the laws provided from equally energized human beings have become primary. We live by the laws of biased opinion rather than laws of truth. Civil Laws tell us what is acceptable and unacceptable, what is right and what is wrong in reference to society. For example, not paying our taxes is not illegal because the Creator says so but because it is the belief of other human beings. These superficial laws have been programmed into the human mind since birth and obeyed due to the fear of punishment from authority figures.

Saint Thomas More (1478-1535), servant of King Henry VIII, was imprisoned because he refused to acknowledge that the King was the head of the Roman Catholic Church in England. When he was given one more chance to acknowledge the King as the head of the Roman Catholic Church before being beheaded, he stated, "Some men say the Earth is round and some men say the Earth is flat, but if it is flat could the King's command make it round? And if it is round, could an act of parliament make it flat?" When Saint Thomas More was making this argument to the court, he was not only testing the common sense of the jurors, but he was also examining their understanding of Universal Law, the order of things, the laws that control authority figures, and the parliament. Despite being beheaded, Saint Thomas More will forever go down in history, remembered as "the King's good servant, but God's first."

Thomas Jefferson also pushed the Universal Laws and inspired individual souls to live their life by these principles. Jefferson stated in the Declaration Of Independence on July 4th, 1776, "We hold these truths to be self-evident, that all men are created equal, that they are endowed by their Creator with certain unalienable rights, that among these are Life, Liberty, and the pursuit of Happiness." When Thomas Jefferson and the Founding Fathers that led the war of succession from Great Britain wrote the Declaration of Independence, they were promising to construct the

United States of America around the principles of Universal Law. Their faith in Universal Law alone inspired the American Revolution and their eventual succession from Great Britain.

Our Founding Fathers deeply expressed that our rights come from our human existence, not from the rights granted to us by other human beings. Rights such as the freedom to think for ourself, freedom to travel, freedom to cherish our individuality, freedom to petition the government, freedom to defend ourself, and freedom to be left alone, if wanted, are all examples of our rights provided by the Creator, God. However, the advanced world of technology has imposed a variety of distractions that blind us to the truth of our natural rights, the truth of our non-physical being, and diminished our higher consciousness.

Consciousness is the most fundamental form of our being; not our bodies. Our body is just an outer image that our soul has manifested into as we experience the physical dimension, Earth. However, we should not live through our bodies, only through our individual consciousness. Our level of consciousness represents our level of interconnection with God. At a stream of higher consciousness, we live through acts of God, living for the love of humanity rather than the illusion of society, directly aligned with the Universal Laws.

Once we understand and apply the Universal Laws, we will have a deeper understanding of how the Universe works. We will have a deeper understanding of why and how we experience the things we do in our daily lives. We will realize that our mind is free, and we have the power to control our human experience. Without the application of the Universal Laws, we are powerless.

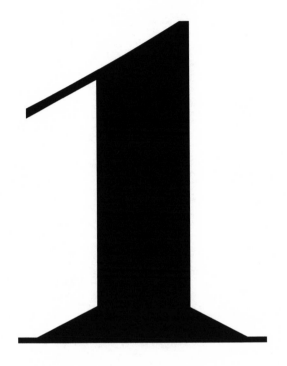

Oneness

"Learn how to see. Realize that everything connects to everything else." — *Leonardo da Vinci*

BOB MARLEY SAID IT THE BEST, 'ONE LOVE.' The message portrayed through Marley's award-winning song was the unification of humanity, a concept that has become extremely foreign to us. We have divided ourselves and look at each other as human beings of different countries of residency, different races, different religions, different political preferences, and different social classes. Instead of coming together and embracing each other as One, we have become blinded by our physical differences and societal labels.

By becoming overly consumed with the illusions of the physical world—television, smartphones, music, cars, houses, marriage, and other subjects that have not always existed—we subconsciously ignore the truth of the vast Universe. The physical world has blinded us to the truth of our existence, which is to experience reality from within instead of labeling external subjects. Experiencing reality from within our being, reaching a state of formlessness—directly aligned with our soul—allows us to interconnect with all life forms, both physically and non-physically. It is in this state of formlessness that we awaken and apprehend that separation is an illusion created by our socially conditioned thought process.

Truthfully, everything is one. Everything comes into the physical world through the power of the same Source, the Creator. This Source remains within each of us, beyond our physical bodies, keeping us all molded together as One on our journey through the human experience. Until we open our mind and accept the truth of Oneness, we will continue to believe that what we have experienced is all the Universe has to offer.

We have to open our mind and understand that we are one in the same as each wave in the ocean and each blade of grass. The more we believe that we are separate from the waves in the ocean and the blades of grass, the more threatening the world will become. It has become easy for us to pollute the oceans and accept the process of deforestation because we are not conscious of Oneness and the interconnection of each living entity. We are not consciously aware of the fact that we receive oxygen from both the ocean and the trees, making it impossible to exist without them.

All things are comprised of the same foundation of energy at the subatomic level—the level of energy within, beneath the atom. It is at the subatomic level that the concept of Oneness exists. A higher level of consciousness, our inner God, can also be discovered at this level. Sadly, many individuals will admit that God—a singular divine power—made the world, but will not admit that the **Powers of God** have been manifested within them. Individuals that neglect to see and feel the presence of God within them and every living entity have fallen victim to the external world, living life from a stream of lower consciousness.

In addition to our individual consciousness, there is a collective consciousness. The collective consciousness creates an invisible field that surrounds the Earth and pours out into the Universe. This field of energy is referred to as the Unified Field, also known as prana, chi, or life force energy. We can access this field of energy by silencing our mind, typically in the form of meditation or prayer. When we silence our mind, we reduce the number of electromagnetic signals sent out to the Universe, allowing us to align with the concept of Oneness residing deep, within our being.

Albert Einstein, the greatest scientist to ever walk the face of the Earth, also supported this as truth, dedicating his life to proving the concept of Oneness. Einstein's well-known equation e=mc2 (energy equals mass times the speed of light squared) was not created to solve for 'e', but instead to solve for 'm.' Einstein eventually came to the conclusion that not only mass is created by energy, but all things both physically and non-physically are created by energy. His most famous quote, "I want to know God's thoughts; the rest are details," was a reference to the Universal Mind, the mind of God, the Creator. As Albert Einstein continued to learn about this formula and discover the truth of Oneness, he eventually coined the Unified Field Theory.

Regardless of our race, religion, gender, social class, and country of residency we are all conscious beings made of the same substance of energy beyond our physical forms—human bodies, animal bodies, leaves on plants. Our lives will take on a more peaceful and prosperous way of living once we realize that where we differ from each other is not in consciousness, but in our distorted ways of thinking, conditioned to look at each other for our physical differences and societal labels rather than feeling that we are all the same by looking each other in the eyes. Collectively awakening to the truth of Oneness will allow the evolutionary process of our species to continue; it is of supreme importance.

"WHEN WE DIE, OUR BODIES BECOME THE GRASS, AND THE ANTELOPE EAT THE GRASS AND SO, WE ARE ALL CONNECTED IN THE GREAT CIRCLE OF LIFE."

— *THE LION KING (MUFASA)*

Vibration

"Everything in life is vibration."

— *Albert Einstein*

EVERYTHING THAT EXISTS IN THE UNIVERSE, both physically and non-physically, is constantly flowing in the form of energy, vibrating and traveling in a repetitive circular motion. Most subjects appear to be solid from the human perspective, but they are not, they are vibrating. The cars we drive, the clothes we wear, the food we eat, and the bed we use to sleep are nothing more than vibrations that we have attached labels to.

VIBRATION

Every subject in existence has a unique vibrational frequency, which explains why everything appears to be different from the human perspective. These unique vibrational frequencies give us an idea of reality, however, the only reality is the one our brain manufactures. Our brain receives millions of signals each second, organizing them into various holograms that we define as reality. Instead of perceiving the signals sent to our brain as singular dimensions, we perceive them as solid objects. By attaching labels to external subjects—blue, red, dog, cat, car, house, and other words we use to describe distinct vibrations—we do not realize that reality is not external of our being, but completely inside of our mind.

Our physical senses of seeing, smelling, feeling, tasting, and hearing exist for the sole purpose of interpreting the vibrational frequency of various subjects. We see because our eyes translate vibration. We smell because our nose translates vibration. We feel because our fingers translate vibration. We taste because our tongues translate vibration. And we hear because our ears translate vibration.

According to head and neck surgeon, Dr. David D. Caldarelli, the human ear can register sound waves with a vibrational frequency of 20-20,000 cycles per second. Sound waves vibrating close to twenty cycles per second have a low pitch, and sound waves vibrating close to twenty thousand cycles per second have a high pitch. However, as humans we cannot hear everything. Any subject vibrating lower than twenty cycles per second or higher than twenty thousand cycles per second cannot be heard by the human ear. Physical objects such as tables, couches, and doors vibrate the slowest, which explains why we cannot hear any sounds resonating from them unless they come in contact with an external source. For example, we cannot hear any sounds resonating from a door until an individual knocks on the door, and we cannot hear any sounds resonating from a chair unless an individual sits in the chair. Once we grasp the concept of our ears translating the vibrational frequency of sound waves, allowing us to hear, we will start to experience life in a more intimate manner.

VIBRATION

Our eyes can register light waves with a vibrational frequency of 430–790 cycles per second. Every color we can see is an expression of white light. The acronym Roy G. Biv represents the portion of the electromagnetic spectrum that is visible to the human eye. These colors are red, orange, yellow, green, blue, indigo, and violet; in the order of lowest to highest vibration. Eventually, the color of violet vibrates into a state of ultraviolet, which cannot be perceived by the human eye.

Since the human form of being is visually oriented and cannot see everything, most individuals deny the fact that non-physical reality—life forms that the human eye cannot see—and vibrations exist. This belief that non-physical reality does not exist also stems from the conditioning of our minds, believing that we only have five senses, allowing us to journey through the human experience on a material plane. However, non-physical reality is where our soul resides. It is where our soul existed before it manifested into our physical bodies, and where our soul will return once we experience death.

Just as everything in the physical world is a vibration, we each have our own individual vibrational frequency, symbolizing who we are to the Universe. Each of our thoughts, words, emotions, actions, and intentions are vibrations that directly affect the level of our individual vibrational frequency. It is important that we become conscious of our thoughts, words, emotions, actions, intentions, and take control of our individual vibrational frequency; it allows us to take control of our life and experiences.

The lower our individual vibrational frequency, the denser our internal energy system becomes, and the heavier our external problems appear to be. When we journey at a low vibrational frequency, we experience pain and discomfort in our bodies, feeling the burden of our emotions. We tend to feel lazy and unmotivated, feeling the need for distractions—cell phones, music, television, and partying—to get us through each day. To live a life of happiness, abundance, and prosperity we must avoid being in low vibration at all costs.

The majority of individuals journey through the human experience in low vibration because of the way the man-made society has been constructed. The few individuals controlling the masses have trapped us into believing that we are nothing more than humans placed on Earth to acquire material—money, clothes, cars, money, and other material things. They constantly fill our minds with low vibrations of fear, ignorance, revenge, and hate. The popular music, television shows, fast food, genetically modified food, cigarettes, fluoride, vaccines, prescription drugs, chemtrails, and media propaganda are all means of corrupting and trapping us into lives of low vibration.

By becoming conscious of these low vibrations and embracing each other with love, we will move into a higher-level of vibration. We will start to experience greater personal power, clarity, peace, and love. We will understand that our emotions are no more than internal energy-in-motion and learn to deal with them easier, feeling no burden from them. Our lives will become full of light, making it easier for us to manifest the subjects that we desire.

Journeying through the human experience in high vibration is essential as we experience troubled times in the world. A world that once understood we are all connected as One has begun to perceive everything as divided, causing many destructive behaviors. Having a high vibrational frequency will naturally cause the vibrational frequency of other individuals to rise, awakening to the truth of their being, realizing that the Earth is an organism that has a vibrational frequency of its own. This has been proven through the studies of James Hutton (1726-1797), the father of geology, describing the Earth as a superorganism, in which is controlled by our individual vibrational frequencies. As everything is One, and each individual relies on the vibrational frequency of the Earth, the Earth also relies on the vibrational frequency of each individual.

The Power of Choice

"IT'S CHOICE — NOT CHANCE — THAT DETERMINES YOUR DESTINY."

— JEAN NIDETCH

Vibrations not only affect us individually, they also affect the individuals around us, the Earth, and the Universe. Each vibration goes out into the collective consciousness and contributes in the increasing or decreasing of the Earth's vibrational frequency, affecting all life forms on Earth. We tend to think that earthquakes, hurricanes, tornadoes, and global warming are natural occurrences, but they only occur due to the low vibrational frequency of planet Earth through the collective consciousness. Taking control of our individual vibrational frequency and moving into a higher-level of vibration will solve the problems of natural disasters, global warming, and world poverty.

The great thing about journeying through the physical world as a being in the human form is that we have the gift of free will. Each of us has the power to choose the thoughts, words, emotions, actions, and intentions we send out to the Universe. Just as we care about our physical appearance by choosing clothes, hairstyles, makeup, shoes, diets, and exercise plans, we must learn to take care of our vibrational frequency by choosing thoughts, words, emotions, actions, and intentions of high vibration. The power of choice is the center of our evolutionary process and controls everything we experience in the physical world. We are decision-making beings; there is not a moment on our journey through the human experience that we are not making a decision.

Each decision and choice we make is a choice of intention that is expressed out to the Universe beyond our being. Once we learn to intentionally make choices of high vibration, we will experience a life of high vibration in return. However, we can only make choices of high vibration by becoming aware of our gift of free will and living life consciously. Regardless if our intentions are consciously intended or unconsciously intended, we have to experience the karma that comes with each choice.

The more unconscious we are about our inner being, the more our intentions will be based upon the part of our being that we focus on the most. Our intentions will come from our ego rather than our soul. For example, the loving part of our being may want to see our girlfriend or boyfriend that has cheated on us become happy without us in their life, but if the cruel part of our being is stronger, we will, with mixed feelings, pray that he or she gets cheated on in their next relationship. If the cruel part of our being is stronger, we will experience the karmic consequences of our cruel intention.

We cannot choose our intentions consciously until we become conscious of our inner being, and the positive and negative dynamics of the individual we have become on our journey through the human experience. If we are unconscious of our ego, we will contradict our inner being by intending one thing and another at the same time. We will intend for our life to go in one direction, but suffer the karmic consequences of it moving in another. We have to release our ego and align with the Universe within to master righteous intentions and make conscious choices.

Making conscious choices and accepting responsibility for the choices we make is the key to mastering the level of our individual vibrational frequency. When we measure out the potential consequences of our choices before making the actual choice, we acquire the power to take control of our experiences. Asking ourself questions such as, "What consequences will this choice produce? Am I prepared to endure the consequences of these choices?" will help us make conscious choices and avoid negative karmic debts. Every choice we make to align with the Universe within our being will be rewarded. The Universe always supports choices that come from our soul instead of our ego.

Our ego is the illusionary image we have of ourself that falls victim to the illusion of the physical world, constantly seeking external power. It is the reason we perceive power as external rather than our natural state of being. It keeps our lives stagnant as we journey through the human experience with a low vibrational frequency, seeking success in a world of competition. Once we become conscious of our inner being and align with the Universe within, we will realize that the only measure of success should be our individual vibrational frequency.

How To Raise Your Vibration

1. MEDITATION

Making time to slow down and align with the Universe within is essential. Waking up in the morning or making time before bed to meditate and reset our vibrational frequency is one of the best things we can do to remain in high vibration. When we meditate, our days go by smoothly shielding us from all disappointment and negativity.

2. EXERCISE

Exercise contributes to both raising our vibrational frequency and keeping our vibrational frequency raised. It encourages energy to move through our brain and stimulates the release of endorphins, which are frequency-elevating chemicals.

3. HANG AROUND HIGH-FREQUENCY PEOPLE, PLACES, AND THINGS

The less time we spend on negative energy, the better. We must protect our vibrational frequency by surrounding ourself with people that are sources of positivity and light. There is nothing better than putting time and effort into individuals that have similar passions and interests, encouraging our spiritual growth rather than discouraging our spiritual growth.

4. BECOME AWARE OF THE FOOD YOU EAT

Becoming aware of what we eat is extremely important when it comes to keeping a high vibrational frequency. Food is an energy source in itself and has the power to increase or decrease our vibrational frequency. Avoiding processed foods, canned foods, soda, fast food, microwaved food, genetically modified food, and artificial sweeteners will contribute greatly to our vibrational frequency.

5. BE COMPASSIONATE

Being compassionate is all about putting positive energy into our lives. One of the highest vibrational frequencies in the Universe is the vibration of love and compassion, making us a magnet for both positive relationships and positive experiences.

" THE HUMAN BODY IS MADE UP OF ELECTRONIC VIBRATIONS, WITH EACH ATOM AND ELEMENTS OF THE BODY, EACH ORGAN AND ORGANISM, HAVING ITS ELECTRONIC UNIT OF VIBRATION NECESSARY FOR THE SUSTENANCE OF, AND EQUILIBRIUM IN THAT PARTICULAR ORGANISM. EACH UNIT, THEN, BEING A CELL OR A UNIT OF LIFE IN ITSELF HAS THE CAPACITY OF REPRODUCING ITSELF BY THE FIRST THE LAW AS IS KNOWN AS REPRODUCTION-DIVISION. WHEN A FORCE IN ANY ORGAN OR ELEMENT OF THE BODY BECOMES DEFICIENT IN ITS ABILITY TO REPRODUCE THAT EQUILIBRIUM NECESSARY FOR THE SUSTENANCE OF PHYSICAL EXISTENCE AND ITS REPRODUCTION, THAT PORTION BECOMES DEFICIENT IN ELECTRONIC ENERGY. THIS MAY COME BY INJURY OR DISEASE, RECEIVED BY EXTERNAL FORCES. IT MAY COME FROM INTERNAL FORCES THROUGH LACK OF ELIMINATIONS PRODUCED IN THE SYSTEM OR BY OTHER AGENCIES TO MEET ITS REQUIREMENTS IN THE BODY."

— EDGAR CAYCE

Attraction

"Anything you imagine you possess."

— *Kendrick Lamar*

THE WORLD LEADERS have conditioned our minds to believe that we are powerless. They have led us to think that life is supposed to be a struggle rather than a Heaven on Earth experience. However, why would the Creator manifest our beautiful souls into the physical world to struggle? Truthfully, as human beings we are over a thousand times more powerful than technology and have the power to create our own reality. It is the Universal Law of Attraction that the world leaders attempt to hide from the masses, for it gives us the ability to take control of our lives and experience bliss, abundance, and fulfillment.

Many religious teachings and ancient philosophers across the world preached about the Law of Attraction. The Bible states, "Ask and Ye Shall Receive." The book of the Quran states, "Allah has given you free will." Historic figures such as Socrates, Plato, Martin Luther King, and Gandhi all implemented the Law of Attraction into their life, eventually manifesting their desires. Each of these individuals, along with many others that have experienced success and prosperity, realized that the Law of Attraction is the power given to them from the Creator, God.

The Universal Law of Attraction states that each of us is a living magnet that radiates thought energy. Every subject that comes into our human experience on a daily basis is a direct manifestation of our thoughts. If we desire different individuals, physical objects, and experiences in our life, we have to change the way we think. In addition to desiring different individuals, physical objects, and experiences, we have to expect and believe that our desires will be fulfilled. Over time, the Universe will manifest what we desire into our life.

Our thoughts act in the process of cause and effect; radiating a vibrational frequency out to the Universe, which allows the Universe to respond by sending back equivalent vibrational frequencies. When our dominant thought pattern is positive, we attract positive individuals and experiences into our life. However, when our dominant thought pattern is negative, we attract negative individuals and experiences into our life. By understanding this process of cause and effect, we will take control of our lives and everything that exist in the world beyond our physical bodies.

Along with our thoughts, we have to align our beliefs, emotions, feelings, and intentions with the subjects we desire. For example, if we desire to be rich, but believe and feel that we are poor, we will never become rich. We will never become rich because we are unconsciously telling the Universe that we are poor. Though the vibrational frequency of our thoughts are aligned with the vibrational frequency of being rich, our beliefs and feelings are not, causing the Universe to push us away from wealth. We cannot rely solely on thinking positive about the subjects we desire, we have to believe and feel that we have already acquired them in the present moment.

On our journey to manifesting our desires, we will go through a series of trials and tribulations, set in place to test our faith. If we remain positive during the trials and tribulations, we will move closer to the subject we desire. On the contrary, when we become discouraged and negative about the trials and tribulations we experience, we push ourself further away from the subject we desire. This process is best described as our individual Tests of Initiation.

Through our individual Tests of Initiation, the Creator aims to fill each void in our life that has not been filled with experiences needed to further our individual evolutionary process. Once the void is filled, our vibrational frequency will increase, allowing the particular Test of Initiation to never return again. The Test of Initiations that we surpass will never return into our lives because our soul rises above the vibrational frequency of these tests. For every level of vibrational frequency we achieve, we will continue to experience different tests; the secret is in remaining positive and becoming conscious of the moral of each experienced test.

Each level of vibrational frequency we achieve allows our life to become more joyous, prosperous, and fulfilled. The majority of our lives appear to be going in circles as we experience the same Test of Initiation because we have not mastered the mental and emotional aspects of staying positive and learning the moral of the particular experience. Instead of becoming conscious of the reasons we are experiencing the particular Test of Initiation, we begin to feel helpless and victimized by life, causing us to settle and continue resonating on the same level of vibrational frequency for the rest of our life.

Settling for a life of low vibration leads to a life full of distractions. Distractions of television, smoking cigarettes, partying, constantly on our phone, and listening to music blind us to the level of our individual vibrational frequency. By distracting ourself we have no control over our mind, and without controlling our mind, we disable our ability to create the life we desire through the Law of Attraction.

Subconscious Mind

"WHATEVER WE PLANT IN OUR SUBCONSCIOUS MIND AND NOURISH WITH REPETITION AND EMOTION WILL ONE DAY BECOME A REALITY."

— *EARL NIGHTINGALE*

Many psychologists have proven that our mind is split into three parts—the conscious mind, the unconscious mind, and the subconscious mind. The conscious mind is responsible for our logic and reasoning. The unconscious mind stores memories of the past and discloses our ability to recall upon them. And, the subconscious mind comprises of the accessible information we have stored through past experiences and acquired knowledge. Each distinct part of our mind has an immense effect on the way we experience the physical world.

Our conscious and subconscious mind resides on the outer layer of our brain, working together to create our physical reality. To learn something new, we rely on our conscious mind. We have to consciously learn the alphabet, learn to swim, learn to tie our shoe, and learn to walk before it becomes an automatic behavior. It is our subconscious mind that allows the repetition of these behaviors to become automatic. Everything that we allow into our conscious mind is accepted by our subconscious mind, ultimately controlling the way we journey through the human experience.

Adolf Hitler, Nazi Leader and mastermind behind the Holocaust, had an extraordinary understanding of the subconscious mind and its application of repetition. It is through this understanding that he conditioned the Germans to believe what he wanted them to believe, eventually convincing them that the Holocaust was a beautiful strategy to start their plan of taking over the world. He programmed their subconscious mind with slogans, huge signs, posters of himself, and mass flags everywhere throughout Germany. Powerful slogans such as, "Today we run Germany, tomorrow the whole world," were said and heard every day by millions of individuals. This led the Germans to believe that they were the superior race, as they eventually started to take action in proving it.

Despite the negative acts Adolf Hitler brought into the world, it cannot be argued that he was one of the most powerful individuals to ever walk planet Earth. Ironically, all of his power came from his understanding of the subconscious mind and its application of repetition. He understood that every thought and belief vibrates and attracts circumstances and experiences of a vibrational equivalent. He understood that the subconscious mind has no ability to reject, accepting everything we feed into it, rather it be positive or negative. Whatever gets into this part of our mind directly effects our actions, experiences, as well as our individual level of vibrational frequency, and Hitler was aware of this.

The mastery of the subconscious mind is what allows us to create our own reality through the Law of Attraction. Many ancient philosophers believed that our subconscious mind is interconnected with the Universal Mind—the Mind of God—blessing us with anything we desire on our journey through the human experience. It is as if we have unlimited power like the superheroes we watched on television when we were growing up. Yet, most individuals are unaware of the subconscious mind and its unlimited power, causing them to journey through the human experience believing they have no control over their lives. They believe that they must conform and follow the norms of society or their life will be miserable. However, the power of the subconscious mind was granted to us from the Creator for the simple purpose of keeping us from being miserable on this journey as a being in the human form.

To avoid being miserable, we have to reprogram our subconscious mind through the process of autosuggestion. Before we can use autosuggestion, we have to become a continual observer of our dominant thoughts. When we are experiencing self-defeating, negative thoughts, we have to replace them with uplifting, positive thoughts. By doing this, we neutralize our negative thought patterns and prevent them from taking hold and increasing the rest of the hogwash we store into our subconscious mind.

The purpose of autosuggestion is to convince our subconscious mind that what we are thinking is the truth. For example, if we desire a new car, we can tell our subconscious mind, "I have a new car." However, manifesting our desires through autosuggestion takes time, so it is important to stay consistent and feed our mind autosuggestions multiple times each day until our desire is manifested into our physical reality. It is an extremely difficult process, but like everything, the more we do it the easier it becomes. Once we take control of our mind through the process of autosuggestion, we will take control of our life.

As human beings, we have the power to create the life we dream of through feeding our desires into our subconscious mind. It is a gift given to us as a part of our current level of evolution. We should never feel the need to live a life that does not make us happy. Our souls have been manifested into the physical world to experience happiness, love, and abundance; nothing else.

"*NEVER SURRENDER YOUR HOPES AND DREAMS TO THE FATEFUL LIMITATIONS OTHERS HAVE PLACED ON THEIR OWN LIVES. THE VISION OF YOUR TRUE DESTINY DOES NOT RESIDE WITHIN THE BLINKERED OUTLOOK OF THE NAYSAYERS AND THE DOOM PROPHETS. JUDGE NOT BY THEIR WORDS, BUT ACCEPT ADVICE BASED ON THE EVIDENCE OF ACTUAL RESULTS. DO NOT BE SURPRISED SHOULD YOU FIND A COMPLETE ABSENCE OF ANYTHING MYSTICAL OR MIRACULOUS IN THE MANIFESTED REALITY OF THOSE WHO ARE SO EAGER TO ADVISE YOU. FRIENDS AND FAMILY WHO SUFFER THE LACK OF ABUNDANCE, JOY, LOVE, FULFILLMENT AND PROSPERITY IN THEIR OWN LIVES REALLY HAVE NO BUSINESS IMPOSING THEIR SELF-LIMITING BELIEFS ON YOUR REALITY EXPERIENCE.*"

— *ANTHON ST. MAARTEN*

Final Words

Please, fight for yourself and your individuality. Fight for what you believe and know that there is no such thing as a right or wrong belief. Fight for what you love, but never let that love overshadow the love you have for yourself. Stop giving into every regressive temptation, because it kills you on the inside. Know that once you accomplish the finding of yourself, you become powerful among all barriers, internal and external.

Please, surround yourself with those who know the beauty of their individuality—the wise, the awakened, and the loving. Stop shunning the people who are true to themselves and speak the truth without fearing criticism. Stop calling people crazy and hear them out; listen to the conspiracy theorists.

Please, start making your life about service and seek the beauty in all things because the universal higher power, the Creator is with everyone and everywhere. Challenge yourself to have an impact on someone's life forever, not just to change their mood for a short period of time.

Please, seek freedom and happiness before you seek anything else. Know that what you are seeking is already seeking you and that you will recognize it when the time is right. Remain awake, always reflect, and always watch. Live your life with love and care, not with greed and unawareness. Live in the way of the light and the light will start to grow in you.

Please, start making a commitment to yourself every day and have enough respect for your being to put your heart into everything you do. Never back down from any obstacle because they are placed on our journey to test our strength and make us stronger. Always acknowledge every achievement you achieve on a daily basis and always think yourself worthy of all things.

Please, stop letting money control your life. Money takes you away from your true love and fulfillment for humanity.

Please, stop idolizing and seeing celebrities as supernatural. They have the same power we have within and are used to distract, dissuade, and deflate our individual point of views of ourself. Their lives are full of fake love, fake beauty, and fake happiness. Yes, they are worth a lot of money, but they are receiving the money to fetishize materialistic and conspicuous lifestyles, keeping money in circulation, helping the producers remain rich and the consumers remain poor.

Please, make it a mission everyday to awaken your soul and not be poisoned. Aim to break free from the mold of society and appreciate the little things. Appreciate the things that are real and genuine, the things you cannot buy. Open your mind to the beauty in all things and all people. See things from different perspectives, but also question every bit of information you come across, and always spread knowledge. It is knowledge that has the power to change the world.

Please, do not let cell phones and televisions become your only outlet to the world. Put down your phone and spend more time being aware your thoughts. Spend more time reading and less time gossiping. Spend more time with nature and less time on the Internet. Stop using social media with the intent to make your life seem perfect when perfect does not exist. Use social media to spread truth, to support others, and for positive community influence.

Please, stop treating reading as a hobby and start treating it as a necessity. Know that reading has the strength to fulfill where we lack and to improve our revolutionary instincts. Learning and growing should be an everlasting daily concept. Do not rely solely on the formal education system to acquire knowledge; the formal education system will only teach you what it wants you to know.

Please, read this book whenever you are having a difficult time and remember that I once had my back against the wall. I fought every day to finish this book with the intention of helping an individual as beautiful as you push through each struggle. To remind you that nothing is more important than our soul, and no external figure should blind us from that. Share the knowledge in this book with every heart and soul you come in contact with. This is a beautiful way we can collectively change the way of the world in a positive manner.

References

Introduction:

The Science of Human Evolution." YouTube. YouTube, 11 Jan.
    2015. Web. 5 June 2015.

University of Colorado Denver. "Evolutionary increase in size of
    the human brain explained: Part of a protein linked to
    rapid change in cognitive ability." ScienceDaily.
    ScienceDaily, 16 August 2012.

Braterman, Paul S. "How Science Figured Out the Age of Earth."
    ScienceDaily. ScienceDaily, 30 Oct. 2013. Web. 28 Oct.
    2014.

Hagen, Edward H. "Why Couldn't Humans Have Evolved during
    the Last 10,000 Years?" University of California, Santa
    Barbara, 1999-2002. Web. 8 Dec. 2014.

Hancock, Graham. "Are We About to Experience a Shift in
    Collective Consciousness?" YouTube. YouTube, 14 Dec.
    2012. Web. 4 Jan. 2015.

"Global Resources Stock Check." BBC. N.p., 18 June 2012. Web.
    5 Feb. 2015.

The Open Secret

Moretti, Marco. "Interview on Psychosynthesis with Roberto
Assagioli." Youtube. Youtube, 27 Feb. 2011. Web. 13 Oct. 2014.

"Polyosophy – Ancient Greek Conceptions of Love." Polytical. N.p.,
    4 Feb. 2012. Web. 9 July 2014.

Harding, Burt. "Setting Yourself Free." YouTube. YouTube, 11
    July 2014. Web. 5 Apr. 2015.

Self-Perception Is Everything:

Branden, Nathaniel. The Six Pillars of Self-Esteem: The Definitive
    Work on Self-Esteem by the Leading Pioneer in the Field.
    N.p.: n.p., n.d. Bantam, 1 May 1995. Web. 18 June 2014.

Don't Doubt You:

Branden, Nathaniel. The Six Pillars of Self-Esteem: The Definitive
    Work on Self-Esteem by the Leading Pioneer in the Field.
    N.p.: n.p., n.d. Bantam, 1 May 1995. Web. 18 June 2014.

"Cold War & Conformity, 1946-1960 Primary & Secondary Source
    Articles." Cold War & Conformity, 1946-1960 Primary &
    Secondary Source Articles. South Allegheny School
    District, 2015. Web. 3 Mar. 2015.

Ferry, Tom. "Why Do We Care What Others Think? Our Addiction
    To The Opinions Of Others Explained." Huffington Post.
    Huffington Post, 17 June 2011. Web. 28 Jan. 2015.

What Aretha Franklin Really Meant:

Branden, Nathaniel. *The Six Pillars of Self-Esteem: The Definitive Work on Self-Esteem by the Leading Pioneer in the Field. N.p.: n.p., n.d. Bantam, 1 May 1995. Web. 18 June 2014.*

Gauthier, Julianna. "Self-Respect - How to Gain It and Why It's Important." *EzineArticles.* N.p., 11 Oct. 2011. Web. 16 May 2015.

Never Stop Evolving:

Rohn, Jim. *"Increasing Your Value." YouTube. YouTube, 11 May 2013. Web. 12 Aug. 2014.*

The Universe (Laws):

Kotsos, Tania. *"The Seven Universal Laws Explained." Mind Your Reality. N.p., 2013. Web. 13 Nov. 2014.*

"Universal Laws Are The Key To Living A Life Of Abundance And Happiness." *Abundance and Happiness.* N.p., 2002-2005. Web. 11 Feb. 2015.

Napolitano, Andrew P. "The Natural Law as a Restraint Against Tyranny." *YouTube.* YouTube, 19 Nov. 2014. Web. 2 Dec. 2014.

Oneness:

"Oneness (Proved by Albert Einstein)." YouTube. YouTube, 11
    Nov. 2013. Web. 2 Dec. 2014.

"The Universal Law Of Oneness." The Metaphysical Society. N.p.,
    n.d. Web. 27 Apr. 2015.

Vibration:

"Superorganism." DBpedia. N.p., n.d. Web. 25 Oct. 2014.

"Food with a High Vibration Which Results in a Higher
    Consciousness." Astounding Elements. N.p., n.d. Web. 3
    Jan. 2015.

Attraction:

A Single Brain More Powerfull Than All Computers Ever Made.
    N.p., 14 Sept. 2003. Web. 10 Jan. 2015.

"Law of Attraction--Collection of Teachings from 10 Amazing
    Speakers." YouTube. YouTube, 7 Feb. 2014. Web. 13 Mar.
    2015.

Carey, Benedict. "Who's Minding the Mind?" The New York Times.
    The New York Times, 30 July 2007. Web. 9 Feb. 2015.

25627442R00120

Made in the USA
Middletown, DE
05 November 2015